# The Masquerade of the Ball
## no more suffering in silence

CINDY HEBERT

WESTBOW
PRESS®
A DIVISION OF THOMAS NELSON
& ZONDERVAN

Copyright © 2019 Cindy Hebert.

All rights reserved. No part of this book may be used or reproduced by any means, graphic, electronic, or mechanical, including photocopying, recording, taping or by any information storage retrieval system without the written permission of the author except in the case of brief quotations embodied in critical articles and reviews.

WestBow Press books may be ordered through booksellers or by contacting:

WestBow Press
A Division of Thomas Nelson & Zondervan
1663 Liberty Drive
Bloomington, IN 47403
www.westbowpress.com
1 (866) 928-1240

Because of the dynamic nature of the Internet, any web addresses or links contained in this book may have changed since publication and may no longer be valid. The views expressed in this work are solely those of the author and do not necessarily reflect the views of the publisher, and the publisher hereby disclaims any responsibility for them.

Any people depicted in stock imagery provided by Getty Images are models, and such images are being used for illustrative purposes only. Certain stock imagery © Getty Images.

All scripture quotations taken from the King James Version of the Bible.

ISBN: 978-1-9736-6160-3 (sc)
ISBN: 978-1-9736-6159-7 (e)

Print information available on the last page.

WestBow Press rev. date: 5/22/2019

## *Acknowledgment and Dedication*

This book is first and foremost dedicated to my Lord. It is His story, love, grace and forgiveness that even makes this possible to be written.

To my loving husband, partner for life, and biggest fan, Jason. This is our story that testifies of the love, strength and commitment that our marriage has to truly endure "for better, for worse, for richer, FOR poorer, in sickness and in health" until death do us part. Thank you for loving me BIG through it all and always believing in the real me! SHMILY!

To my boys, Parker and Peyton, I love you both and will always be your biggest fan. Thanks for being mine through this process. You were my reasons for even trying to get well at the beginning and I hope you take from this testimony that you are both strong enough to dream big and achieve it with God's help and guidance.

To my family, thank you for being patient with me for so many years and for loving and praying for me. All of you never gave up on me and you tenderly guided me back to finding myself.

To all those who suffer with depression and/or anxiety, don't let Satan steal your joy-just keep fighting!

And this book is written in memory of my mom also known as Nana by the world that loved her dearly, I kept my promise, I am okay!

# Contents

Acknowledgment and Dedication ........................................................................ v
Introduction ............................................................................................................ ix
        Why a Masquerade?

Chapter 1 ................................................................................................................ 1
        The Story Behind the Mask

Chapter 2 ................................................................................................................ 7
        Choosing a Mask or Did It Choose Me

Chapter 3 .............................................................................................................. 17
        Losing Myself Behind the Masquerade

Chapter 4 .............................................................................................................. 23
        Wear It Well

Chapter 5 .............................................................................................................. 37
        Behind the Smiling Mask

Chapter 6 .............................................................................................................. 47
        Not Hiding from Everyone

Chapter 7 .............................................................................................................. 77
        Forced Freedom

Chapter 8 .............................................................................................................. 91
        Mask Drop

Chapter 9 .............................................................................................................. 99
        Mask in Hand

Chapter 10 ..................................................................... 111
        God Didn't Create Masks, So Be Bold!

Chapter 11 ..................................................................... 125
        Blinded by the Masquerade

Chapter 12 .................................................................... 135
        You Choose

Chapter 13 .................................................................... 153
        The Mask Isn't Worth It

Chapter 14 .................................................................... 157
        The Music Plays On

## Introduction
## Why a Masquerade?

Labels are put on everything from canned goods to our clothing sizes and even our own identities. Labels are affixed to things as a way of describing someone or something and used as an identifying marker. Labels are necessary but can be detrimental when we place them on ourselves. Many times, the true identity of someone becomes hidden behind the label. It doesn't change the outcome whether it is placed there by another person or by ourselves. Fear sets in when our true identity doesn't match the label and the expectations that accompany them. In the secular world, this is considered false advertisement.

Living a life of false advertisement is easy to do when fear of becoming discovered as an imposter is always at the forefront of your mind. Many years of living a lie, hidden behind a label and not even knowing what reality was had become the standard in my life. I wanted many times to rip off the labels placed on my life like little children pull them off canned goods out of mischief or boredom. Moms must play a guessing game when they choose a can, and I too wanted people to have to guess and accept who I truly was without the labels. Unfortunately, that was not possible. I had built a life around a false identity. I lived in silence screaming to let the real me out with the pile of thick labels stacked on top of each other. These labels, created by others and myself, are what caused me to begin wearing a mask. The pressure to maintain my created identity, as I had become known as, was insurmountable.

That is the life of wearing a masquerade. A cover-up living with a smile plastered on my face, doing what was expected of me, living as I was told and never wavering from the identity that I had created. That is a huge weight I placed on myself that only lead to detrimental consequences. Many may be shocked as they read the details of my past. This is not about how bad things had gotten in my life or how well I had hidden all the very low times. My story is to break the silence about depression and anxiety and the reality of both. My story is about addiction. My story is one of hope and healing. My story needs to be heard because labels are more than just words on a tag of clothing or a soup can. But you see all of this is not just my story, it's God's! It is a hefty pressure to live, be, and act in a certain way according to some unwritten standards. So, here's to ripping off that label and being real.

# 1

## The Story Behind the Mask

Each intricate detail was strategically chosen with the best of intentions to woo them all. Many continuous hours of shopping took place to purchase just the right wardrobe. She needed to have the exact one to compliment her hair, skin tone, and figure. It took thought, planning, and searching many hours on her tired feet walking from store to store to find the picture-perfect look made just for her. Not only was the outfit a must, but the right shoes to compliment everything was mandatory! They couldn't be too high because her feet would hurt instantly, but they couldn't be too low because she didn't want to give off the impression that she was old and frumpy. So, they too were purchased with the intent of making a lasting first impression on those that she saw that night. The make-up and hair ritual was altogether different. She didn't trust anyone but herself to make her appearance flawless for the big evening. Each stroke of lipstick and eye shadow had been applied very strategically with the utmost of precision and the best of intentions to cover any imperfections or blemishes that may be there. The details needed to accentuate all her best features cohesively. See, she was going to an event like no other. She was going to a ball! It was a special event, and she wanted to be noticed and to stand out in the crowded room.

She had only one opportunity to stand out at the ball, and she was going to make it perfect. However, perfection always comes with a price. A price of countless hours of preparation to make sure nothing goes wrong. It was a strategy that she had calculated in her mind over and over to make sure nothing was out of place or forgotten, and each detail was impeccable. She wanted just the right lasting footprint and memory to be left on each person she encountered that evening. She wanted no one to know that she was wearing a masquerade at the ball. No one must know the real her and what was hidden behind the mask of well-applied makeup and the fake smile that extended from ear to ear.

It was imperative to stand out. She must be special, and she must be noticed. The outward appearance is a picture of perfection. It shows no flaws, weaknesses or imperfections and certainly never wavers or gets tired. It was as if her appearance had been photoshopped. She was only allowing others to see what she wanted them to see. Perfection! Having it all together, at all times, with everything neatly in place, and no detail was ever forgotten. It was a daunting and exhausting task to keep up this facade.

Perfection comes at a price. It became a price of mental and physical exhaustion over the role-playing each and every day to maintain the persona of what she wanted others to see. This ball was like no other. After all, it wasn't just a ball, a onetime event or another special occasion, it was her life. She was free to choose any masquerade to hide behind. She chose perfection each time and every day, but it was taking a toll on her and for those closest to her. Her time was literally consumed with keeping up the appearance of flawlessness and having no faults.

Her life was not realistic, and neither was this masquerade. Everyone was dancing in slow motion around her. She became just a bystander. She was no longer enjoying the party. The mask that she had been wearing for many years was disguising her true identity to all those around her. Those in her inner circle, and deep down in her own heart, were the only ones that knew who was truly hiding behind the masquerade.

The music had already stopped playing and the ball was over, but the vicious cycle of wearing the masquerade continued day in and day out. It was no longer just situational. She knew if she removed the disguise it would expose every hidden blemish buried deep down inside of her mind. She could not cope with the thought of her identity being exposed and her frailties being revealed. She must continue with the masquerade, just as she had learned to do.

So, with calculated strategy, the daily struggle continued with every situation and with each interaction and relationship. No matter the exhaustion or cost it was taking to keep it up and maintain it, it must continue. The masquerade was now not only reserved for special occasions but had become a permanent fixture to hide behind. She now had to keep up the appearance she had created so everyone would continue to believe and recognize the one they thought they knew.

Her masquerade wearing had become so normal and natural that she lost the memory of her true reflection when she looked in the mirror. The days turned into weeks, the weeks into months, and months turned into years of wearing the masquerade at the ball she called life….13 years to be exact.

So why not just take the mask off? The faint memory of who she was before the masquerade had faded away and she no longer knew who she was without it. It had become her identity, her job, and consuming her life. The lipstick smile was painted on each and every morning and being a pillar of strength had become a performance role that she acted out in every situation.

She knew she could never remove the masquerade because of the frail and fragile little girl hiding behind the mask. She was scared to say no, to ask for help, or to show that she didn't have it all together all the time as she appeared. If the world knew what was under the disguise it would shock them and devastate her. It had become an exhausting chore to keep up the appearance. The thought process of performing a role had vanished and the act had become a natural thing for her. She knew no other way, and there was no escape.

Would she ever truly dance again in this life without the masquerade? Could she ever reveal who was hidden behind the costume? Would the music at the ball continue to play and the party carry on without her? And could she ever really be herself, taking part and being happy, being her true self in this ball called life without the masquerade?

After a big awards show, we all know critics are eager to criticize all the wardrobes that were so carefully selected, purchased, and worn. Participants are then placed on the "Best and Worst Dressed" list according to someone else's standards. That is very similar to the way my life actually was. I was on the "Best" list and didn't want to hit the "Worst." Others are so quick to remark to "just be yourself, and be who

God created you to be." However, it was too overwhelming to suddenly change from the person I had led everyone to believe I was for so long. It was not as simple as a wardrobe change. Grasping the process that it would take to change my identity to those around me was frightening. That stirred enough fear inside of me to keep up the masquerade I had created for myself to wear and maintain on the "best" list.

To announce my hidden identity was not like joining a witness protection program or moving away and starting all over as someone else. I would be literally changing myself and who I had become to all those I came in contact with day in and day out. It would also be discovering my real identity. Because of wearing the masquerade for so many years, I no longer knew who was truly looking back at me in the mirror from behind the mask. I had forgotten and lost all identity of myself and through time the role had become dictated to me by those around me. Society mandates different roles for different people. I was convinced that each role, in my life, being a woman, a mother, and a Christian, and further adding the stipulations that are secretly written as a preacher's wife, compounded expectations that I felt I had to maintain with perfection. I no longer knew my true self, but just the person I appeared to be.

In some form or way, we all wear a masquerade. We cave in to peer pressure, insecurities, and fear and then conform to be who others want us to be. I laugh when I think of the things children have said to me in the past in daycare work or the way a two-year-old throws a temper tantrum and we are all appalled by it. I never got offended by a young child saying I was fat or looked pregnant. They are innocent and haven't learned to filter their words yet. I often say, when a child is throwing a fit and others are appalled by it, that they are acting and doing things that we as adults wish we could do or say. The only difference is that we adults have learned to "conform" and control our emotions in an appropriate manner.

But this conformity in my life had reached an entirely different league. It took self-control and bridling my tongue to a completely different level. It takes molding and conforming to a different level of being strictly who others wanted and expected to a point of completely losing who I really was. It was a role...a charade...a masquerade. There was nothing natural nor healthy about it. I had become a stranger to my own self after blurring the lines of reality and masquerade wearing for so many years.

Is it possible to really be true without the masks? Yes! I didn't realize it nor believe it! The Bible clearly states that "I can do ALL things THROUGH Christ which strengtheneth me." (Philippians 4:13) You must make a conscious choice each and every day to be you. I thought it was too hard. I cared too much about what others thought. Recognizing and believing the thought of living as who my Creator created me to be was foreign to me, but the words were easy to teach to others. Losing your way is so easy and finding it is even easier, but I just didn't know how. I didn't know how to break the cycle and take the mask off. I knew Christ as my personal Savior, but I didn't have an intimate relationship with him where I believed or trusted in Him for my daily struggles. Others may not understand the "mask-less you" because they may have never seen who is truly under there, to begin with. That certainly was the case for me.

It is always interesting to me when someone wears a specific uniform day in and day out for their job and then you suddenly see them in a different setting out of uniform. You stare and stare trying to figure out who they are and where you know them from. Sometimes we don't even recognize them, but we know we know them from somewhere. We drive ourselves crazy trying to figure out who they are. The same principle applies here.

The mask is off! You begin a new walk in your life in a different way. The location of the ball is the same, but the way that you dance, the way you dress, and the way in which you act will all be different. So, look at yourself with new eyes and listen to the beat of the music that your Master is playing. Know that no matter what the other attendees say about you, the hidden person behind the masquerade that decides to just take off the mask will find that it is liberating and freeing. It is a weight taken off that you were never created to bear. Wearing a masquerade through this life that I am considering a ball is not worth it. I wish I would have learned many years ago how to take off the masquerade, let my hair down and just enjoy the music playing.

## Choosing a Mask or Did It Choose Me

As a little girl, I have always been fascinated with makeup and dressing up. My mom never left the house without being completely together, not even to Walmart, Dollar General or Big Lots. Hair fixed, makeup on, clothes ironed, if needed, and jewelry to make the outfit complete. Each piece complemented the other perfectly. The jewelry was always the icing on the cake just to compliment all the other components. She would not have been caught in a store in pajama pants or yoga pants and we all know you had to have on clean underwear just in case of a wreck.

Makeup became an integral part of my young life as a little girl. I can always remember watching how meticulous she was at putting it all on and how beautiful she was when it was all completed. She was not finished until the last stroke of lipstick was in place. Then and only then was the task complete and she could go about doing her daily business. I learned a pattern. Don't go in public until you have it all together!

PUBLIC SERVICE ANNOUNCEMENT!! Don't shut the book now and think that I had a horrible childhood. Don't think that I am going to blame all my problems in life on someone else and that I was a victim. That is not where I am going with this!

Mom would meticulously prepare her face daily with first washing it, then applying the toner and rubbing in the moisturizer on her face and neck. Then the concealer was applied to cover up any imperfections that might be showing. The foundation or base was the next layer just matching the skin with the appropriate tone and color that was not too dark or orange. She did not want to look like she had put on self-tanner or had been in a tanning bed too long. She certainly didn't want to hug someone and leave a stain on their shirts.

Next, the powder was placed to set the base, carefully applying the blush just along the cheekbones and then the eyeshadow color was selected. She would pick just the right one to match her outfit but not that crazy sky blue from the '80s because the latest trends were not always classy. She would select the color to match her outfit but making sure she did not look like a clown. Her eyeliner was placed just slightly in a line but making sure she did not look like a "Jezebel." Her mascara was brushed on and occasionally her eyebrows were darkened when the need would arise. Lastly, the lip liner and lipstick were applied.

Mom did not feel dressed unless just the right shade of lipstick was applied with very careful attention. It was a daily routine for her and a habit for life. I have often said, jokingly of course, that if Mom could have gotten her hands on a tube of lipstick on her deathbed she would have.

So how quickly I picked up that routine as a little girl. Little girls sneak into their Mommy's bathroom cabinets and drawers hurriedly smearing on lipstick and clumping mascara all along their eyelids. They have no clue the proper placement or technique needed to apply it correctly. All they dream about doing is what they consider is needed to become a beautiful woman. Beautiful like their Mommas.

Wearing makeup is a rite of passage to finally becoming a woman, just like our Moms, so that we can be beautiful like them too. We consider it a milestone transitioning from a little girl to a young lady. This is the time when we finally get our own set of makeup and our own responsibilities to make ourselves up to be beautiful just like her.

When that day came for me, I can remember that my Momma had a lady come to our house that worked for a reputable makeup company and she taught me how to properly apply each step. My mom said if I was going to wear it then at least I needed to know how to accurately put it on and to take it off. It was a privilege for me to wear it and she did not want me going out of the house looking unkempt or like a woman of the night. That's how I learned my first beauty tips. I paid close attention to every detail that was being taught to me that day. I felt as if I was learning the coveted secrets to be a beautiful woman by covering up any flaws and dressing up my face just right.

I learned how to get it all together before facing the world. My mom considered always being completely dressed and everything together as a sign of self-pride and self-respect. She was proud of who she was and wanted to present to the world that she cared about herself and was confident. I, on the other hand, took that to a completely different level. My mom never intended for me to literally apply this concept to coping with life. I certainly do not blame her or anyone, for that matter, for my own internal struggles.

Then we add a completely different dimension to further complicate things, that I have ALWAYS been a people pleaser even at a very early age. I never wanted to disappoint my parents, friends, or anyone for that matter. I can remember being so hard on myself about my grades that nothing, but straight A's were acceptable. So, there are parents reading this right now who are saying, "What's so wrong with that?" There is nothing inherently bad about that thought, but the internal turmoil and drive that I would put myself through were not healthy.

I remember my very first F on a test in 5$^{th}$ grade. It was so impressionable and scarring that I remember each and every detail. Back in those days, you had to have papers, especially bad grades, signed by your parents then returned to the teacher. I walked to and from school and was probably on the verge of a panic attack on my way home over my bad grade. I had to take it to my parents to be signed and return the next day. I decided to throw it into the drainage ditch on my walk home. I could not bear the thought of facing my parents with my first failing grade. Well, of course, I got caught when I never returned the signed test and the teacher called my Mom. I then got in trouble twice as bad both for the grade and the lying. I was unrealistically worried at a very young age that my parents would be disappointed in me. I couldn't bear the thought of someone thinking less of me or thinking I was anything but the best.

Then, I can remember another occasion with my grades that caused me to have major anxiety. It was my first B on my report card, and I remember it like it was yesterday. It was also in the 5$^{th}$ grade. I guess that was a hard year for me. I stopped by the bathrooms at school before

I headed home. I was so sick to my stomach with worry that I had diarrhea. I was filled with complete worry and panic on the way home carrying that report card with that single B glaring at me the entire three blocks home. In a panic, I once again decided to throw it in the same drainage ditch not remembering my previous punishment. I was just overwhelmed that I was not thinking clearly or about anything else but getting rid of what I considered a failure. My parents were strict and knew my capabilities and this grade would have been acceptable to them; however, I had placed very unreal expectations on myself. I had created fictitious consequences up in my head for not measuring up to the perfect scale I had designed for myself.

Fast forward as a young adult, anything less than perfection is what caused some of my depression early on. I was scared of failing and scared of not being loved if I made errors or mistakes. I had put so much pressure on myself to be perfect and was afraid of failing or looking weak. Satan had planted that root of perfectionism in my life at a very young age. For many years, that root grew and embedded deep. Habits formed with countless actions to make sure that I would be perfect, put together and strong, or at least appear that way. This way of life I had created caused more problems than I could comprehend.

Throughout my young adult life, it grew out of control like the kudzu along the side of a mountain. It just took over and the deep seed of insecurity was born and carried over into all areas of my life. I was never truly at peace with myself and never found healthy coping skills when I did make a mistake. I just keep putting on the masquerade and placing myself in situations to not allow myself to fail no matter what. I never gave a second thought to the fact that it didn't matter how concealed I thought that I was keeping my emotions and insecurities, God knew.

Marty Rubin states that "Behind every mask, there is a face, and behind that a story." I just didn't want anyone knowing mine and did what I thought was necessary to make sure that it did NOT happen. In 1 Samuel 16:7 the Bible tells us, "...look not on his countenance, or the height of his stature; because I have refused him, for the Lord seeth not as man seeth; for man looketh on the outward appearance, but the Lord looketh on the heart." I knew that verse, taught that verse, but I never took that verse into real account in my own life. I never realized that God saw the real me. I had everyone fooled into believing my masquerade including myself.

I also recall being very detail oriented as a child. There is nothing wrong with being thorough, but I used my perfectionism habits on a totally different level. When I went to the doctor or the dentist, my mom would have to tell me every detail of what was going to happen. I wanted no surprises. I wanted to know every instrument being used and its purpose. I wanted to know what was next and why. It was a compulsion that caused anxiety.

Now, I know many people would dismiss this as being inquisitive and detail driven but to me it was control. If things were not done just as my mom had described or told me then I would panic. If things didn't go exactly as I was told, then internally I would have issues and anxiety would build up. I would then stress during the entire process. I now realize that control was a major factor in my anxiety issues. Those of us who struggle with control issues have a mindset of the way things need to be and wavering from that pre-planned idea will cause stress.

In my childhood, I began habits that seemed harmless at the time and just dismissed them as my "personality trait." But it spiraled, without me realizing it or recognizing it, and it became a much bigger problem the older I got. I learned to put on that masquerade in all areas of my life. Once I was of age and given permission to wear makeup, I did it every day. As I went from childhood to adolescence, I also learned to "put on" makeup every day in every area of my life. I would put on that mask. I would not allow myself to show any negativity or weakness thus never learning to deal with my true feelings. I would keep negative emotions suppressed and tightly covered up by my beautiful layers of makeup and my Brazen raisin lipstick that outlined my smile.

I caught on quickly by forming habits of looking beautiful on the exterior all the while thinking that the inside would take care of itself. I felt it was personal and hidden and no one needed to know about my secret junk anyway or to be bothered with it. I learned people pleasing meant I had to look the part even if my heart was struggling or raging. It was hard to maintain and had become a daily chore. I would make sure that I looked beautiful on the outside as a ritual preparing for my day paying careful attention to every detail. I would pick out the right outfit and finish it off with the perfect jewelry. But all the while I neglected my inward struggle that had been compiling for years.

The people pleasing intensified into my teen years and I learned that I could find security in numbers. I quickly began to feel as if I always needed a boyfriend who would validate my self-worth and could give me undivided attention. I never grasped the truth that I was "fearfully and wonderfully made." (Psalms 139:14) That was me all by myself without a plus one. I never learned that my identity was defined by Christ and who He created me to be. I didn't understand or comprehend that my identity and self-worth had nothing to do with me. I could not grasp the fact that no matter what I did or didn't do that God loved me the just the same with a perfect love.

I can remember a vivid memory of my high school years driving around the mall for fun. I spent countless hours and many tanks of gas driving in circles as friends would wave, play loud music and just yell mindless hey's and hi's at each other. We were all aiming to claim some kind of status in our group and to be noticed apart from the crowd. Everyone knew about this one special guy that drove a black Camaro and had dark opaque tinted windows. It was a dream car and he would roll his window down about half way. All you could see was his piercing blue eyes and flowing beach blonde hair. He was so mysterious and magical to all the young teenage girls. He came to be known and nicknamed by the girls as "Mr. America."

Weekend after weekend, Mr. America became the sought-after guy and each girl would jockey for his attention. It became a challenge for my group of girlfriends to see who could get a date with this guy first. As we drove round and round weekend after weekend, one night of circling changed the mindless driving for me.

That particular night I had three girlfriends in my car, and we decided to make a challenge between the 4 of us. We wanted to see which one could get a date with Mr. America first. Of course, I was driving so I had the advantage. I saw his car pulling around the mall corner and I knew it would be my night. I slowed my car down as he passed by and I hollered at Mr. America. Yes, not quite on the top of the list for awesome flirty techniques, nonetheless, I hollered, and I yelled, "Hey pull over," and he did!

# THE MASQUERADE OF THE BALL

Mr. America pulled over in the Sears parking lot and slowly got out of his car and strolled over to me. I felt as if he was approaching me in slow motion like the lifeguards running on Baywatch. I was finally getting a glimpse from head to toe of the mysterious guy that all the girls had been dreaming about. He was a gorgeous guy, according to a young teenage girl's standards, and he was talking to me. After an hour or two of talking and my friends googling and giggling in the background over him, he asked me out on a date. Yes me, he asked me. I won the bet!

Fast forward to date night as I fretted and changed wardrobes 10 times wanting to look my best. Each outfit that was rejected was now laying all around my room. This was my one chance to go out with a guy like him and I felt like I could ruin it with making a rookie mistake like picking the wrong outfit but finally settled on one. Then I applied my makeup, picked out my jewelry and sprayed my perfume. Then I brushed my teeth for a second time just in case.

As I was peeking out my front window, I anxiously waited for his arrival as he slowly pulled into my driveway. I was excited and nervous all at the same time. Not only was Mr. America at my house to take me on a date but he was driving his magazine worthy Camaro. I felt like the luckiest girl in the world. He came to the door to get me, as all nice gentlemen do, and walked on my side of the car and opened the door for me. We were just making casual conversation and I thought to myself, "What a gentleman!" I felt at that very moment that he was the whole package. It was the icing on the cake- handsome, cool, and had date etiquette! I believed it was going to be the best night of my life!

Well, my date story isn't quite over, and I am sorry to spoil it, but it didn't have a magical fairytale ending. All I can say is the rest is history. He took me to the movie theater and the movie we wanted to see was sold out. He then decided to take me to get something to eat. He was such a gentleman every time getting in and out of the car opening my door ever so carefully to allow me to exit the vehicle. Our conversation was usual for a first date of just getting to know each other as I was trying not to talk too much and to stay engaged in the conversation.

We pulled into the restaurant for dinner and it was a Taco Bell. Not only was Taco Bell our dinner, but it was the *entire* date. We sat there for three hours while he waited for all his friends to meet him there and to hang out. They were all at the movie that we were supposed to see but didn't. I learned quickly by this date that some things are not always as glamorous as they appeared to be.

See it was the challenge between the girls and the excitement of winning Mr. America's attention that was the true thrill. But the end result was nothing more than the heartburn and gas from a three-hour dinner date at Taco Bell. The date was not what I had dreamt it to be nor was going out with a coveted guy. Neither made my status amongst my peers any better. I was searching for a position among the girls. I wanted them to be jealous, but a supreme taco and nachos bell grande are nothing of which to be envious of.

Searching for self-worth in other people will only leave you disappointed and disillusioned. It will create an overwhelming feeling of never truly being satisfied. The internal struggle with control and my self-worth issues only left me empty and deeply disappointed time and time again. I did not realize that I was placing a responsibility on other people that they were never intended to have. I was disillusioned that my self-worth was validated by other people. It was hard to maintain my perfectionism to impress others. Having to know every step in my life had become a power struggle and a deep-rooted lack of faith.

Defining my identity was never intended to be my job nor responsibility. The years of trying to cover up my internal war and trying to control everything around me with a perfect mindset quickly became too much for me to bare and my mind and heart grew weary. The masquerade of having it all together all the time was beginning to weigh too heavy and the music at the ball of my life was spinning like a broken record and not even one that I liked. The masquerade that I had created for myself was beginning to close in on me. I couldn't last much longer and at this pace. I was just too tired of faking it.

The problem escalated when the masquerade could no longer be taken off. It had become fashionable and fun to wear at times. Yet, I had created a monster that could not be stopped. I had taken on so many flawless attributes in all areas of my life. The "perfect" persona, that I thought I had, and that people had come to know, was expected from me. I had set a high standard for myself and others knew me according to that perfect performance that I had always given. I started checking and rechecking everything that I did constantly for imperfections. I would always make sure everyone was happy and going to any length to assure that was possible. I had developed such unhealthy habits in my life and in my relationships that the joy of the ball, which was my life, had ended. Life was no longer fun to live and had become a chore.

Fear began to creep in, and it made me second guess all my decisions no matter how many times I checked to make sure every detail was covered. The fear of someone being disappointed or thinking any less of me than perfect was overwhelming which then produced anxiety. It was a grueling task and a long road to haul all that baggage. I could not keep up the marathon race in my life and it had to come to a stop one day. No one is designed to maintain a level of perfection that I was trying to maintain. It just isn't realistic.

I was not only trying to deceive everyone around me that I had no imperfections, but I was also trying to deceive myself. I lived a lie each and every day putting on my masquerade. It had now become a permanent fixture. Jesus was and is the only perfect one, but that did not resonate with me. The Bible verse that states "Who did no sin, neither was guile found in his mouth," (1 Peter 2:22) was a frustration to me because I thought that somehow in a disillusioned, sinful way, that it was describing me.

I had everyone believing just as I had wanted them to. The masquerade was working, and everyone believed it, or did they? See I had become too tired of keeping up the charade and act. I had begun to slip up and I had to take the mask off at some point and the only ones I could do that with were the ones closest to me. The ones who would and could keep my little secret, my family! My disguise was not working at home. My family would see the unfiltered version of the frail person behind the masquerade. They saw the raw, tired, and frustrated person that had been pinned up with stress, fear, and anxiety. That is how the vicious cycle began. The masquerade would come off and the enjoyable dancing music immediately stopped in the privacy of our own home.

# 3

## Losing Myself Behind the Masquerade

Webster defines "intention" as a determination to act in a certain way. I never intended to be the way that I had become. I was not determined nor set out to be a monster at home or to break into fits of rage or crying hysterically for no reason. I believe in the deep crevices of every person's heart, that is of a right mind, is a pure intention of not deliberately setting out to hurt another person. I hated who I had become. Hated the fits of rage that would make me spew curse words and call my husband ugly names. I hated the person that would take a decoration in our bedroom and chunk it across the room putting a hole in our bathroom door. I did not like this person, nor did I recognize her. No one outside of the walls of our home had met her. Each time that rage would well up inside, it felt as if someone or something else would just take over. It felt as if the tantrum was an out of body experience. I needed help!

I needed someone or something to stop all the anger, anxiety, and fear. I could control all of it in public around everyone else, but I could not tame the rabid dog that was out of control in our own home. The emotions could no longer be suppressed. After each episode, I wouldn't even remember what I had said, but I always knew it was bad and I would see the aftermath of destruction both in the words and in the faces of those that I loved. I had to apologize over and over and pick up all the broken pieces of both the objects that were thrown and the hearts that got torn apart from my disaster of emotions that were projected onto them. My husband, Jason, was usually the one that was almost always in the path of my destruction.

The fits began very innocently with a normal frustration of things not being picked up or a messy house. I would be upset over the feeling of being underappreciated. There were normal marital issues, but they were so minute in comparison to how big of an effect that I allowed it to have on me. I created high levels of stress for myself and had become an emotional roller coaster, out of control, and off the tracks. So, I finally broke down and decided to go to the doctor which was against everything I believed or wanted, but I needed to be on my A game all the time and the music was skipping beats pretty often at my ball of life. My mask was starting to lose the elasticity that was holding it on around my head.

I went to my friendly general practitioner that I saw for sore throats and migraine headaches. He asked me lots of questions and I answered them honestly. I felt a slight weight lifted off of me from the burden of hiding because I could finally honestly verbalize my frustrations. I didn't feel the need to sugar coat things or maintain my cover up with him because I knew there was a patient-doctor privilege and he couldn't tell anyone. He told me the words that I did not want to hear. "You're depressed!" Ok, I can deal with that as he explained that sometimes hormones in ladies and chemicals in our brain get out of whack and maybe I needed a little something extra to help with that.

He comforted me with the same words that I would hear over and over through the years, "Depression is a medical issue. You wouldn't dare ask a diabetic not to take medicine or if your leg is broken you surely would not choose to not put a cast on it. Sometimes you need medicine to help stabilize the chemicals in your brain that are no longer working as they should." I knew the stigma in the Christian world concerning the usage of depression medications and he convinced me with his comforting words that this is what I needed to do to heal my brain and my emotions. So, I started my first depression medication about 2001.

It was a very low dose and it was only taken around my cycle because that was when my emotions were the craziest, so surely it was hormonal. My first diagnosis or label was Premenstrual Dysphoric Disorder. All it meant was I was really moody around my cycle. So, I took it the week before, the week during and the week after so that only left one week out of the month with no medication. After six months of taking the medicine, I realized things were not much better, and there were only six total weeks of non-medicine taking over that half of the year. I was still having sporadic emotional issues that were very intense, so I felt that I needed something more to help me change.

Surely, there had to be something else wrong with me or maybe I needed a little something extra. So, the doctor then placed me on a different antidepressant, but still a very low dose. I always felt as if my doctor had my best interest in mind and trusted him. I mean surely the statement that I heard so many times before, "We all can benefit from taking a little something" is true, right? That statement put me more at ease as depression medications were now being prescribed to me to take on a daily basis. That statement could be considered true for most of the population to be happy, but not for a control freak, perfectionist with a type A personality that always wanted to please others. Admitting that I had any weakness was incomprehensible and very hard to deal with each time I swallowed that antidepressant pill.

So as the new medicine got more and more into my system and the suggested two weeks went by, the good days were becoming better and the bad days, well I hate to say, were still really bad. It was always extremes. I found myself sleeping a lot. I was then surprised and excited that baby number two was on the way in 2003. I was taken off the depression medicine immediately. The rages and down days all came back with a vengeance. After the first trimester, my doctor placed me on a very safe dose of an antidepressant again, so that I could cope and function, day to day, even while being pregnant.

I began to have some serious pains and complications around my fourth month of pregnancy and the doctor discovered a large cyst on my ovary. Cysts usually dissolve or are absorbed into pregnancies but mine was not and was continuing to grow. My ob/gyn was concerned that it may cause complications with the baby; therefore, decided that I needed to have surgery to have it removed.

During my preoperative visit, my doctor repeatedly assured me that he was going to stay away from our baby boy when removing the cyst. I wasn't quite sure how that was possible, but his confidence created a sense of peace in me. By law, he had to go through the required and routine list of scary details and complications that could occur, but he ended all statements with the reassurance that the practicality of risks was minimal. I understood them completely and signed all my pre-op paperwork in his office. As I signed the consent, I silently prayed. I prayed for God to take care of me and my baby boy.

Fast forward and now surgery day was here. I have had a few previous procedures before, so I knew the basic routine of having surgery and what to expect in the operating room. I knew the temperature sticker was placed on my forehead and my arms were strapped down while all the monitors were being placed on me. I knew that it would be meat locker cold and the nicest nurse in the world would come and lay those coveted warm blankets on me quickly. As each one of those things was completed by the nurses and staff as normal protocol, I was prepared and expecting each step up to this point.

The anesthesiologist then came into the room. He stood to my left towering over me with his blue scrubs on from head to toe. He asked me the very routine and almost robotic question that I had heard before, "What are you having done today?" I responded with the very non-medical practical answer, "I am having a cyst removed off of my ovary." But then he replied in a statement that still fills my ears and sinks my heart each time I think of it, "You know you are going to lose this baby." I didn't answer him because I was assuming he was just going through the protocol and making me aware of the risks that could occur. I didn't think anything strange nor did I answer him at that point and was thinking that he was just doing his job.

So, I then decided to answer him back in a shaky but now nervous voice as I began pondering his statement, "I know the risks, Dr._____ told me that he was going to stay as far away from the baby as possible." As I was breathing into the oxygen mask getting prepared to drift off to sleep hoping that our conversation was over, he then reciprocated in a mean and unsympathetic tone hiding behind the surgical mask, "You are going to lose this baby." Tears began streaming down my cheeks as I drifted off to sleep.

I am blessed and pleased to tell you that I did not lose my baby that day and Peyton is now a teenage boy, but what I did lose was courage and all peace of mind. That encounter with being completely out of control and being faced with something devastating, defenseless against all odds, and helpless was the birth of my new battle with severe anxiety.

I, by no means, validate what the doctor did and understand that they are required to make patients aware of risks that may occur, but it was the manner in which he went about it. At my post-operative appointment, I made my doctor aware of what had transpired in the operating room and he filed a complaint with the hospital board.

Anxiety according to Webster's dictionary is defined as, "fear or nervousness about what might happen or a feeling of wanting to do something very much." I can tell you not only had I begun a battle of depression in my life that was having more low days then high, but that experience lit a fire of anxiety in my life that began to rage. Now I was battling two mental illnesses that were deeply rooted in control issues. My anxiety was birthed and lived completely in the what if's and the maybe's.

I know scripture tells us not to worry and specifically in Philippians 4:6 states, "Be anxious for nothing, but in everything by prayer and supplication with thanksgiving, let your requests be made known to God." At this point in my life, I believed that verse was only speaking about the really big issues in life and that complimented my view on most Biblical issues. I excused my own struggling convictions by validating that I was not responsible for my actions; therefore, not accountable for not applying the beliefs and principles directly to my life. Subconsciously, I would just add my own interpretation of the verses to justify my own feelings and actions.

"Be anxious for nothing," for me, meant to control everything so you won't have those feelings or a reason to be concerned. Well, the part about prayer and supplication was an admirable habit but I believed that God was not interested in hearing my mundane complaints and stress over my outfit, or the mess in my kitchen or having just the right lessons prepared. My thoughts were that true dependence was reserved for the big life-changing decisions not the day in day out redundant living problems as a mother and a wife. I didn't want to waste God's time on the daily humdrum things that stressed me out and made me anxious.

So, the mask became a more permanent fixture because I couldn't allow those around me and especially those in the church to know that the preacher's wife was having all these problems. I believed that I could not stand before the kids and ladies and teach if they knew, so I camouflaged the truth. The depression and anxiety had become my dirty little secret and I was proud that I hid it so well. But once again, not from everyone, my family knew. My husband knew all too well when my hair wouldn't fix just the right way and I would yank the hot curling iron out of the wall and throw it. My boys would know that each toy in their room had a specific spot and when that was not followed through correctly or sorted in the appropriate containers, they would suffer from my stressed out, hurtful words.

    I felt as if my cover up and mask were all pretty and put together. My ball was carrying on to some beautiful Christian music, of course, but my heart was disintegrating inside of me and I could not let anyone know. No one must see the woman behind the smile, behind the makeup, and the outfit picked out with purpose. With Bible in hand, I carried on.

# 4

## Wear It Well

Self-examination is hard to do. No one wants to look in the mirror naked. Most don't even like to look at themselves fully clothed. I am not just talking about the physical examination, but also emotional and spiritual. Nobody wants to accept or admit any personal weaknesses and certainly don't want to own up to them. We don't like to confess to ourselves much less to anyone else. Therefore, we look into the mirror with a preconceived judgment of what and who is staring back at us.

Sometimes if we stop and truly take a self-inventory, we don't and won't recognize the person staring back in the mirror. We know who we think we are or who we are supposed to be and so, therefore, that's who we see or what we have allowed others to see. Our true identity is not recognizable through the lens that we are often looking through. The masquerade has us nicely hidden. Rose colored glasses are how we often look at ourselves. All pretty and pink yet not seeing the thorns!

Time went on, if I had no meltdowns and stayed in control of my emotions, we considered that a good day. I tried to maintain my persona of mom and wife of the year and volunteered to be room mom for my son's classes. I stayed up all night crafting those little seasonal gifts and snacks to make sure those little kids' faces would light up when they received them. I had to find things no one had seen before, and they had to be perfect. If not, they were trashed, and I started them all over. I had to make sure when and if they took them home to their parents that they were just as wowed with my creations of the Valentine pudding robot or the Halloween popcorn monster hands that I had stayed up countless hours crafting.

I never did anything halfway and wouldn't ever consider the thought of buying something store bought. Those small snacks and handprint Thanksgiving placemats had to be over the top and perfect so they would be forever etched in their little memories when they looked back on their preschool years. The Halloween monster cake for the cakewalk at the carnival had to be "the" cake that everyone was talking about and wanting to win. I know this may sound ridiculous to you, but I was not thinking rationally during this time. I was living with an unrealistic perfectionism life motto that was unattainable and I was not living in truth or reality.

The good days were really good and small glimpses of the real Cindy would come out, but the dark days continued to be really *really* bad. The vicious cycle would go back and forth. The dark days were filled with anger, crying, panic attacks, yelling and lots and lots of blaming. At this point, I had developed a habit of running to the doctor on those bad days. I went back and forth to the doctor each and every time and explained to him about the roller coaster of emotions that I was going through. Finally, a real "diagnosis" was made. I finally had a "reason" for all my unexplainable and uncontrollable behaviors that no one could fix or tame. As the doctor said the words, "You are bipolar."

Well, that was not what I was expecting and something foreign to me because I had no clue what it meant. He explained to me that it was mood swings between being really happy and then really sad. It was explained to me that some people go years in between swings, some people have seasons, and then some people swing daily and many times throughout the day. Well, of course, that was the category that I felt that I fit into. I had multiple mood shifts within each day. So, I felt relieved that I had a diagnosis to explain WHY I WAS THE WAY I WAS.

This is what I wrote in my journal on October 26, 2005.

> *Well, today I heard the words that I never wanted to hear. You have bipolar disorder or manic-depressive disorder. No matter how you say it, it is ugly. I never wanted this, I don't*

*want this, I just want to be normal. Whatever that is! I was put on 40mg Geodon and 40mg Prozac. You think that's enough! Jason has been really quiet about the whole thing. I feel sorry for him and what he has had, is and will have to put up with. Now that I have had my pity party, next I am a little happy that I have been painfully honest, and I can learn to deal and manage it. Small baby steps! I just don't want people to look at me and always think is she high or low or what mood is she in. I just want to be me!*

I was placed on my first mood stabilizer, in addition to the anxiety and depression medications, because what I was previously taking was not enough. I stayed depressed and anxious most of the time. So, I began the frequent routine of going back and forth every few weeks for checkups to my doctor. He explained to me that it took about two weeks to see the full effect of the medicines allowing them to get into your system enough to see results.

I would always get impatient wanting an immediate fix and I would burn up Hwy 7 heading back to the doctor before the two weeks was up with a list of complaints and issues. I had an explanation of why I thought this medicine isn't working and insisted that it wasn't fixing things and allowing me to function like I wanted to. My doctor would then increase my dosage or switch medicines altogether. Within a seven month time span, I had almost tripled my anxiety medicine going from one milligram to 3 milligrams of Klonopin.

Now that I had my diagnosis, I could excuse and explain why I was the way that I was. Bipolar disorder had become my masquerade to now hide behind. I would validate my behaviors saying that I couldn't help it and telling others that they just didn't understand what life is like living with a mental disease. In March of 2011, I started my first blog called "The Buzz on Bipolar." I have always had a deep desire to help others even while I was struggling. I wanted to share some excerpts from that blog for you to understand my mind frame and how those who seem to have it all figured out can deceive themselves and others by wearing a masquerade.

## The Buzz on Me and My Mission

*Hi!!! My name is Cindy Hebert and I have Bipolar with Anxiety Disorder. However, that is just my disease not who I am. I am a Christian, a Mother of two boys, a Sister, a Daughter, and a Preacher's Wife. Most of all I want to be a friend.*

*I love my life, but there are things that I don't like. I will share with you the ups and downs I have had dealing with both disorders. They are not a death sentence like I used to think, and they really can enrich your life if you learn how to use your positives and not the negatives.*

*I have not always felt this way and I want to take you on my journey as to how I came to think that way and the major struggles I have had in the past. Through all this God, my family, and my church have been by my side. I will share with you my life transparently.*

*By my saying all of this, I want to be a friend and a help to others who are struggling with some of the same issues. Maybe it is just depression, maybe it is the loss of a loved one, maybe it is just anxiety, but all of these can be an overwhelming cross to bear. I am by no means a doctor, a counselor, or an expert. I am just me with real-life experiences that have changed my life.*

*God is my doctor and His word is my supreme expert. I haven't realized for many years, and really not until recently, have I realized that at all. I have always been a pessimist and I am becoming more of an optimist with the Lord's help.*

*I chose the Buzz on Bipolar because I love bees. Not because they are busy and making sweet honey. In all reality, they can be awful pesky. No pun intended. A bee is not naturally or aerodynamically created to be able to fly, but they do. God created them too!! So, they do, and they do it often. Their main purpose is to fly and make a better environment for others, like flowers. I want to be a BEE!! I want to be exactly what God created me to be*

> and to make my environment better. I am not referring to reduce, reuse, and recycle. I am referring to making my own life, my family, my church, my community, and my world a better place with God's help as He would have it to be. Even having Bipolar.
>
> So, stay tuned to the BUZZ, on the life, of a child of God with Bipolar.

I began to sleep a lot, which can be, a side effect of the medication or it was just my way of escaping life altogether. I would often excuse all the sleeping and mandate that it was normal bipolar behavior. I would justify my actions to get out of doing things as a lack of capability or drive for doing it because I was bipolar. It had become my go-to as my script that I used often. I acted out irrationally at times because I was bipolar so it must be a swing, right? I am sleeping a lot because I am on a downward swing, right? I have to take so many medications because I am bipolar, right? I am happy and exceptionally creative and crafty because I am manic because I am bipolar, right?

I always had sincere intentions deep down inside. I was trying to appear to have everything together even with the beginning of the medicine pile-up cycle. Down in my heart, my motive was pure and positive. In this past journal entry, you can see that I was most concerned with what others thought.

> It then began to be a roller coaster of cycles of meds to try to get things under control. On October 26, 2005, I heard the awful words, "you are Bipolar with an Anxiety Disorder." I was shocked. The doctor was great, and he tried to explain to me what was going on with the cycles of mania and depression. No matter how he explained it. It was ugly. I thought that only crazy people were Bipolar. I thought I don't want this, and I want it to go away.
>
> I wrote in my journal that I was embarrassed by it because I didn't want people thinking "is she high" or "is she low" and wondering what to do around me. I just wanted to be normal whatever that looked like!!!!

Something that always bothered me deep inside, and now I realize, is when I would read about bipolar, and boy would I read, I would read that a manic swing would exhibit behaviors that were irrational and grandiose. That the person would exhibit feelings of being a superhero or wanting to conquer the world. Many people spend tons of money, become sexually promiscuous, or do unexplainable behaviors that can be harmful to themselves because they have no fear or reality during a manic episode. Yet, all I ever did was craft A LOT and have trouble sleeping. I just felt maybe I didn't have a bad case of bipolar as if I was comparing it to a case of chickenpox. I never questioned my doctor because I just wanted an explanation as to why I was the way I was. I wanted a fix to make it all better and if that was not possible, I needed an excuse.

I can remember one Christmas family get together that we were all sitting around laughing and playing games and midafternoon medicine time came. I jumped up from the living room couch as if there was a fire because I realized that I had lost track of time and ran and took my medicine. I then left the family fellowship and went and took a nap, because "my meds made me tired."

I left without explanation and didn't excuse myself from the activities. When I woke up and the family had wondered where I had gone, I just replied, "It was the meds!" But I felt as if no one understood and that they were always judging me about my struggles. I felt that they didn't know what was going on inside my brain and certainly didn't have a doctor's degree to say anything contradictory. I trusted my doctor and believed my diagnosis, therefore, I fully lived out my diagnosis and continued taking all my medications.

A habit according to Webster's dictionary is "a usual way of behaving: something that a person does often in a regular and repeated way." So, there are good habits and there can be bad ones too. I had developed a habit of running back and forth to the doctor every time I had a bad day. When I felt as if I wasn't myself or I just couldn't cope, then down that highway I would go to the see my doctor. I would explain with a dramatic attitude, explicit details and utter desperation, that the medicines aren't working again, or they were not enough. I would convey to him that things were just not right, and I couldn't cope with life and many days I couldn't function normally.

Surely, he believed that this all stemmed from the disease because I was a Christian, a Mother, and a Preacher's wife who was living right and these behaviors were not me nor who I truly was. I taught Sunday School, a ladies' class, and oversaw the youth. I convinced the doctor over and over that I could not control my behavior and he believed me. He would increase or change my medicines over and over. We were trying to find just the right combination of mood stabilizers, antidepressants, and anxiety medications for me to function and respond to life in an appropriate manner. Yet, when I was out of the confines of my own home and out of our single wide trailer, I was functioning normally for the most part. I knew how to keep things in control and hid.

My masquerade was neatly in place and I was carrying on in my ball of life like nothing was going on. I would carry on at church and school functions just fine but the minute I walked into that white rectangular metal manufactured home, the masquerade came off and all restraint of my emotions was gone. I was drained of energy because keeping up my masquerade and having it all together all the time was tiresome. I would usually be a tornado and rant and rave through the house destroying everything or everyone that came in my path and I had become like a giant stomping on that particle board floor to get my way. I acted like that two-year-old in Walmart that doesn't know how to control themselves because they want candy at the checkout line, but I was a grown woman who the world saw as having it "all together."

After I finished my tantrum, I was exhausted and would just throw myself into bed. I would let Jason pick up the pieces both emotionally and sometimes physically if any items got thrown that day. Lord Byron stated, "And, after all, what is a lie? Tis' but the truth in a masquerade." To the outside world and beyond, I was living a lie. I was also wearing a complete masquerade to the reality of myself and who I was and who I had become. I had hidden behind the diagnosis and the descriptions of how I was supposed to act having bipolar. I continued taking the medicines and making excuses for my behaviors while blaming the disease and never looking at who was truly behind the mask.

My doctor felt as if he had helped me all that he could, and any further treatment needed to be done by a psychiatrist. I made an appointment and vividly remember my first visit in his waiting room. I filled out my paperwork with all the usual generic information that is required. While writing, I was distracted by a lady sitting near me that was talking to herself out loud. There was also a little boy staring off into space and then there was me just sitting there. I was prideful and naive thinking that I was not anywhere close on the spectrum of mental illness severity as them.

I mean no disrespect to anyone with a mental illness and I have nothing but compassion for those who suffer, but that was the deluded mind frame that I was in at that time. I was filled with complete denial and self-defense. I wrote out my long list of medications and those I had taken in the past and was shocked seeing it written out on paper. It was definitely eye-opening how many I had gone through.

My name was finally called, and I went to the nurse's desk to do the normal triage blood pressure and weight stuff and then went into the psychiatrist's office. I was a little nervous and a lot excited because I felt that surely, he specializes in mental illness and could fix me.

I walked into a dimly lit room expecting incense to be burning and for me to lay on one of those couches like you see on tv, but instead, he just asked me to sit in a hard metal office chair just like the ones in the waiting room right next to his huge oversized desk. I sat there for a moment answering very vague questions and then we transitioned with me sitting on the small loveseat and him at his second desk in the room. As I moved, I was hopeful that we would now discuss the really important things and get down to the bottom of all my problems. I thought I would tell him my hang-ups and issues and he would tell me how to fix it. At that time, I did not understand the difference in a psychiatrist and a psychologist. Not realizing that a psychiatrist was a medical doctor that prescribed medications and spent most of the time on management of that, while a psychologist focused on treating the emotions with behavior modifications and intervention. The doctor I was seeing was definitely the first.

I went through my explanation of my actions and reactions very carefully with such desperation that I needed help to be fixed. I felt confident that I was describing to him one of the worst cases he had ever heard, and he was going to make me a top priority on his treatment list or so I had imagined.

He listened then revealed that he didn't want to change too many medications all at once. He said doing that wouldn't help him to find out what was really working and what wasn't.

He then explained that he was just going to order one medicine adjustment at a time, and it could be a long process to find what helped me to function normally. I remember the moment that he said long process I felt completely hopeless again. I even had a thought of not going back to him because he didn't care enough and surely, he wasn't really any good if he didn't have a miraculous combination of medicines. I needed that instant fix or magic pill to smooth it all over and I couldn't understand why he just wouldn't prescribe that perfect one. So, I left there not liking that doctor too much because I felt he did nothing for me, didn't care enough and certainly didn't get me.

The one thing that the psychiatrist did suggest to me was to get into counseling. I started looking up counselors in our area and I knew I had a strong desire to only see a Christian one. I knew I was strongly convicted not to see anyone that would mention or suggest any psychobabble stuff. So, I found someone that met my criteria and I made an appointment. I made arrangements to go and see her before I had to return to the psychiatrist in two weeks. I was convinced by then I would be making progress because I was on the hunt to get well.

It was appointment day and I pulled up into a very neat and quaint part of Nacogdoches, Texas, to a two-story house that had been converted into an office space. I made my appointment later in the evening in hopes that no one would see me there. I felt as if no one could know that the preacher's wife was going to counseling and it was my plan to continue to hide it. It was dusk just before the sun was setting as I pulled in the parking lot. I checked my lipstick in the rear-view mirror one more time to make sure everything looked just right and was in its perfect place.

I was excited and persuaded that this counselor would understand the stressors that I was feeling day in and day out being both a mom and a preacher's wife. I went with a preconceived plan that she would just teach me how to say no, cope a little better, and learn to ask for help from others properly. She may mention that I needed to learn how to loosen my control and just be able to delegate all together. I felt my issues were all wrapped up in a tiny little box and just had to be unpacked like a present at Christmas with each layer at a time. I felt as if I just needed to be taught how to strategize and cope with all my different roles in my life.

The counselor had previously told me that everyone in the building would be gone and to call her when I arrived. So, I did. I gave her a call on my cell phone and told her I was there. She directed me to go to the second floor where her office was located. I walked into the dimly lit house with a small lamp being the only light on in the hallway. The wood stairs were located on the right side of the entryway.

As I began climbing the stairs, butterflies started swarming in my stomach with each step that I took getting closer and closer to the top. At the top of the stairs, I saw a bathroom and I immediately went in. My nervous stomach had hit and now I had diarrhea. This was my usual response when I reached a level high level of anxiety and unfamiliarity. Deep down I felt ridiculous because I knew she wasn't going to hurt me and only help, but anything that was new to me or out of my control made me queasy and sick.

I entered her office. It was a very small space with an old blue floral couch and a small black fridge with a few plants in the corner. She walked into the waiting area after I had been sitting for only a few minutes and greeted me with a warm and pleasant hello and smile. She offered me a drink and quickly said let's get started. She guided me into another room with a large desk, metal filing cabinets and another small metal waiting room chair with black leather. Those chairs must have been on sale somewhere that year since they seemed to be in every office I had been in recently. There was an old ficus tree in the corner and she grabbed another chair from another room for herself. She had a yellow legal pad and a pen in her hands.

She quickly asked me a few formal questions, but then started diving into deep matters. She asked about my spiritual walk and the effects that this was having on me and my family. I felt that finally someone cared about me and wanted to know the real truth. After talking for a while, she assured me that I could get better, but I had to put in a lot of the work. Work! What? The brakes jolted in my mind. It's the disease, I thought the bipolar was making me do all these horrible things, so I just needed to learn how to cope with this hand I was dealt and teach others around me how to help me. I felt slightly offended that she was putting some responsibilities on me and not agreeing that it was just the mental illness.

As the appointment ended, I was slightly more hopeful than I had been in a very long time, but I was still a little apprehensive. I knew she was a Christian and I felt as if she had actually listened to me. I left with a list of scriptures to read and use as my go to when I was having troubles. She ended the session in prayer and made an appointment for me to come again. I left her office that day thinking I felt a little better already and more at peace because I felt that I had found a voice. Someone finally listened to my deep dark struggles and I was relieved that I had a game plan. I knew in the depths of my heart that the spiritual side needed work so seeing her definitely soothed my soul.

Over the next year, I rotated between the psychiatrist and the counselor learning to adjust to new medicines and trying different coping techniques to handle life and stress. In one session with my counselor, I learned how to meditate for the very first time. When she mentioned that we were going to do it, I was a little, or to be honest, a lot leery of it. I felt as if I might be crossing the line in this whole spiritual thing, but she explained and taught me that it was just a discipline of learning to relax each muscle and area of my body. She also taught me during the meditation time the practicality of truly being still. It felt peaceful to quiet my mind for just a brief moment forgetting why I was even there.

My concern over my reputation and testimony was always there and I wanted to be careful about what others thought of me. Even though I was verbally admitting that I had problems in private and needed help but dealing with the root of the problems was a completely different concept. I knew there was a spiritual component to healing, but I couldn't grasp the degree of importance. This excerpt from my personal blog writing, soon after my Bipolar diagnosis, will show you how it is easy to type out and post for the world to see, but a lot harder to take personal responsibility:

> *So, I was diagnosed. There you have it. I was doomed or so I thought. Why me, Lord? What have I done? I will do better. All the while He is saying I chose you, that's why.*

*"I will never give you more than you can handle."* But at that time that was the furthest thing from my mind. I was angry and I was angry at God! I wouldn't admit to it, but I know it now.

*So, I went for years going back and forth to the doctor with this medication problem or this depression issue. I would get so low and deep and dark I couldn't even look up or around me to see the people that loved me and were praying for me. I soon found out the issues with bipolar like feeling good, so you stop medications is very common, but it is very dangerous and not at all the thing to do. I would spiral into depression and then jump into the mania like a rocket full blast. Now I never have had a full manic episode where I do outlandish things. I just have severe insomnia (that soon will cause a migraine) and lots of cleaning and crafting. I am really a creative person during a manic episode.*

*I started going to a Christian counselor after a couple of years and she was great. But I always felt like I heard what she was saying but I couldn't apply it to my own life. "This case is different." "Don't you get it? Christians aren't supposed to be depressed." "I am saved." "I have the Holy Spirit inside of me and I am a Preacher's wife, this isn't supposed to happen to me maybe they are all wrong." All the while I couldn't see my destructive behavior by shutting out my husband and getting so low that I stayed in bed for days without showering or brushing my teeth (gross I know)!*

*I never really got settled in the fact that if Jesus doesn't heal me of this (which was my prayer) I needed to accept it. I wouldn't be alone. But that is what I felt, all alone, for many years. Loneliness is an awful feeling. Even though I had a great support system in my husband, in my church, and in my family, I couldn't let them in because they didn't need to see the real me. So, I hid behind a mask!! Mask no more, I have been freed from that bondage of embarrassment and I wear my cross to bear close to my heart with God's help. We make it day by day!*

Mentally I now felt more in control of things after seeing the counselor for a while and felt as if I was ready to tackle my physical battles. My weight had reached an all-time high and I was continuing to rotate between the latest fad diets and exercising. I never really felt like I could get complete control of my weight. I started researching lap band surgery and found that it was best suited for me out of all the weight loss procedures. I had a few friends that had the gastric bypass or the gastric sleeve and I was not ready for that full commitment at that time. The band would give enough restriction on my eating to limit me, but I would still be able to receive my nutrients from my food.

Of course, insurance did not pay for the procedure, so Jason and I began saving as I met with the gastroenterologist and he explained the requirements and commitment that it would take on my part. I had to have a psychiatrist approval and a recommendation from my current doctor before he would approve the surgery. So, I acquired both and they agreed that this would help me with many different aspects of my life. I was always searching everywhere and in every way for a "fix" to make me truly happy.

Jason and I saved the money in order to pay for the procedure and it was scheduled. We had to drive to Houston, Texas, for the operation and it was an outpatient procedure. The surgery went great and I had high hopes for losing lots of weight, and as a result, my self-esteem rising. I was motivated that this would help me to learn to cope with life and that all my struggles would melt away along with the weight. I did end up losing about one hundred pounds over the course of a year, but unfortunately the problems did not vanish, instead, they compounded.

I was making progress on getting my weight problems under control, but the inside emotions were still in shambles. Wearing the masquerade became harder and harder because I felt as if I should be happier, more confident, and secure in who I was with the recent weight loss. Most people would definitely feel better and have a more positive demeanor in life when losing drastic weight, right? Then why didn't I? I had realized at that point that the issue was not the weight, but rather much deeper and more complex and it was as a matter of my heart. My heart was not where it needed to be so my emotions followed wholeheartedly and most definitely to my detriment.

But once again, only the confines of the Hebert home knew just how detrimental my unstable heart and emotions were. Everyone outside of the confines of our humble abode saw what I wanted them to see. The masquerade strategically placed, painted up with make-up and in position with a smile for everyone to believe that I had it all together all the time. The physical weight may have been falling off, but shedding the masquerade was not something that I was convinced, could comprehend, or even considered doing.

# 5

## Behind the Smiling Mask

Finally getting on the right track with my weight while other things in my life were continuing to derail. My mother's health was failing as she battled with her diabetes, which she had been diagnosed with, around the age of thirty. Around the age of thirty-five, she was placed on insulin and struggled with multiple infections and complications due to the disease which caused her to be hospitalized frequently.

Being the baby of the family, I felt like I needed to be with her every time she was sick even though living an hour and a half away in Texas. Dad needed an extra pair of hands, or so I thought. I wanted those hands to be mine. It was fulfilling to me to be needed. We didn't live too far away so about once a month we would make the hour and a half drive to visit. I always felt the need to check on her, and it certainly continued after each boy was born giving them the blessed opportunity to visit grandparents.

There were a few occasions during the years where Mom was so sick and had to be intubated. I remember this one time driving to the hospital frantically from Texas and the idea of speed limits had become foreign to me. I had one mission on my mind and that was to get to my Mom and be with my Dad. As I entered Willis Knighton Hospital in Bossier City, Louisiana, and pressed the button for the elevator an overwhelming feeling of helplessness consumed me. I was not in control of this situation and I couldn't fix it. I hated that feeling.

As the doors opened to the second floor, I walked passed the ICU waiting room and my Dad wasn't sitting in there. I wasn't startled quite yet because I knew it was almost visitation time. I was confident that I would find him waiting in the hallway at the Intensive Care doors anticipating the time when he could go in to see her. As I walked down that blank white hospital hallway, I felt as if everything was so barren and cold. I knew we had been in this position before and Mom had pulled through and was fine and believed that she just needed to let her body rest and start taking better care of herself.

Dad met me in the hallway and this time he had a different and unfamiliar look on his face. His expression seemed tired and worried and it didn't settle well with me. I hugged him tightly, of course, and immediately started asking questions. Questions that I felt I needed answers to, and I wanted my dad to answer all of them thoroughly. I believed being educated about the situation made me feel less helpless and more in control of something.

Dad began telling me what was going on and explained that her heart was getting weary and her blood sugar was out of control again. But something was different this time, Dad cried. Usually, my Dad was always a picture of strength, as a Veteran, and a soldier for the Lord, but at this moment, he was like I had never seen him before. My dad was the epitome of a loving and caring husband. He explained with brokenness that this might be the time. The time that Mom wouldn't and couldn't pull through.

So as the doors to the intensive care unit opened, I went back to visit Mom. She was hooked up to all the machines and I pleaded with her to rest, but to not give up fighting. She was intubated and sedated so there was no response back from her. I knew she could hear me, so I just kept talking. I caught her up on the boys and all their activities as I gently stroked her arm. I reminded her how much she had to fight for them and for me. I kept trying to encourage her and tell her to get better so she could play army men and wrestling men with my two boys.

I leaned over the tubes and IV lines when visiting hours were ending and told her, "I love you. I'll be back in a few hours." I felt in my heart and gut that she would be okay just like every other time that she was really sick. For my own sanity, I tried convincing myself that my Momma was always going to be there. I believed that was the way things were supposed to be and kept comforting myself with the thought that people pass away when they are old. My momma was only fifty-nine.

We spent that night trying to get comfortable enough to sleep in the ICU waiting room. We rotated between the two-seater chair to pacing the floor. Trying to get out the cramps that were forming from being squished in awkward positions in the waiting room chairs. We did anything to occupy the time between bathroom breaks, getting caffeine and raiding the snack basket that a local church had placed there for families. That waiting room became our home over the next several days. I kept waiting for the moment when Momma was just fine and would be coming home while smiling. She needed to pull through, get well, and hurry back to church to resume her Senior Saints activities and keeping grandbabies.

Now it had been several days that she was on the ventilator and the doctor explained to us that the longer she remains on it the harder it would be for her body to wean off it. But see, I felt as if the doctor didn't know my Momma personally as we did and that she pushes herself. She is a fighter that never complains, and this time would be no different... or so I thought.

But as the days went on, this time was beginning to seem a little different and a lot scarier for me. Mom wasn't weaning off the vent as fast as previous times she had been placed on it and was not responding back to us as quickly. The doctor just kept saying to us that time will tell. I kept trying to stay hopeful thinking and praying each day that I went for visitation times to see her. I tried to always stay upbeat and strong for Dad and for myself. I demonstrated a great amount of strength and control with my emotions during that time, considering the circumstances.

I hardly left the hospital except to go the short distance to my parents' house to shower, eat, and then return before the next visitation time. I don't remember exactly how many days this ritual went on, but hours in between visits seemed like days and days seemed like an eternity just waiting, waiting for Mom to wake up. Finally, they were able to take mom off the ventilator, but she was needing to be transported to a rehabilitation hospital to gain her strength and to maintain her stable glucose numbers.

The day that she was transported to the rehabilitation hospital I remember going to my parent's house and cleaning so Dad wouldn't have to worry about it when Mom got to come home. I wanted it to be ready for her. We went to see her later that evening after allowing her time to get settled into the new facility. When I saw her for the first time in the new facility, I remember feeling slightly disappointed because I felt as if she had not progressed far enough along as I had hoped or envisioned. She had to remain on a BiPAP machine, and she looked so tired and weak. I guess I had hoped that the new environment and transport would have magically made a difference.

For many years previous, Mom had vowed that she never wanted to go on dialysis. Her reasoning behind that decision was that she felt as if people that went on dialysis never make a complete recovery. Unfortunately, she had to start it because her kidneys were failing. Her heart was so weak, and her lungs were laboring. I would continue to talk to her each and every time I went letting her know that it is all going to work out and that she just needed to rest allowing her body to heal, and to build up her strength.

It was time for me to return to our home in Texas and I felt the need to stop and see Mom one last time before I did. Jason and I went in to see her and I just kept stroking her arm as I always did. She would open her eyes momentarily and glance at me from behind her BiPAP mask. Her eyes were filled with desperation and it seemed as if she was wanting to say something to me.

At that moment that is forever etched in my heart and mind, I had a sick feeling in the pit of my gut, and I knew my Momma was worried. She wasn't worried about dying because she knew her Lord as her personal Savior, but she was worried about me. Mom was my go-to person when I felt out of control and hopeless. I could and would pick up the phone to call her and lean on her wisdom and her voice would settle me. She could immediately calm me and keep me grounded when I was spiraling downward. At that moment, she was concerned about us, about her kids and grandkids. That is just the type of woman, Momma, and Nana that she was. We were all her world. But I knew she was especially worried about me and if I was going to be alright. See, I didn't have to wear a mask around my Mom. She knew the good, bad and even the ugly about me. I called her on the good days, the bad days, and the really bad days. I hid nothing from her as I did from the outside world.

So, I asked Jason to leave the room while I had a heart to heart talk with her. He looked at me with concern and I assured him that I would be alright. As he walked out of the room, I wanted to scream as he crossed the threshold, "Please don't leave." Yet, I knew I needed to have this conversation with her. It is not one that anyone ever wants to have with their loved ones and I certainly didn't want to have it with my momma.

I held her hand and stroked her arm like I had done countless times before as I began to talk to her. I told her that I needed her to listen because I had to say some really important things that I felt she needed to hear from me. Her eyes opened wide as she raised her eyebrows behind her BiPAP mask. I knew at that moment that she understood me and that I had her attention.

With tears streaming down my face, I expressed with only an ounce of courage that I had at the present moment, "Momma, I am going to be ok. I promise I am going to be ok. I will be fine, and I love you. You can go. I will be ok." She looked at me with tears building up in her eyes and gently pulled her hand up to her face.

She moved her mask away from her mouth wanting to respond. Her movements were slow and uncoordinated. She was very sick and depleted of energy. She knew at that moment exactly what she was doing. With strength, confidence, and warmth of my mother's love, she mustered every bit of energy that she had to form the following words with her lips to say to me, "I love you."

I helped her put her mask back on with tears streaming down my face and kissed her cheek ever so gently as I bent across the hospital bed rails. I walked out of her room that night and Jason and I drove back to our home in Texas. I got the "the call" early the next morning. All my dad said to me was that we needed to come NOW as I heard the pain and urgency in his tone, but his information was very vague. I knew it was bad and I felt it in the pit of my stomach. I started throwing clothes in bags and grabbing a little of any and everything that I may need for a long-extended stay again. I felt in my heart that I needed to grab dark church clothes "just in case. "

I felt guilty for even thinking about those things, but I had to be prepared. Jason drove with urgency and silence for the hour and a half drive to the rehabilitation hospital. We walked in the front entrance of the hospital and my dad met us in the lobby waiting area. So many of the consequent details are a blur due to the shock of the moment and the fact that it still feels like a bad dream. Dad told me that Momma had passed on. My Momma passed on to her Heavenly Home on January 30, 2007, and now was experiencing a body rid of sickness and diabetes. With the humor and wit that only my Momma had, she always told us that those people that spent all their lives getting fit and trim were going to be shocked when the glorified body was "fluffy" like hers' and now she had it.

I was in disbelief at first because Mom had many scares over the years when we thought she wouldn't pull through but this time the fear had become a reality. Dad said the nurse walked into her room during normal rounds that morning and Mom was alert and in a cheerful mood. The nurse said mom cracked a joke with her as she was taking her routine vital signs. The nurse walked out of the room and mom coded. After many hugs in the waiting room that morning, I then walked down the long hallway to see her and to pay my last respects. It was one of the most difficult things that I have ever done.

The next day our family went to the funeral home and discussed service arrangements, I felt as if we were discussing things for someone else. Reality had not hit me at that point. I did know the only requests Momma had were that there were to be no red roses and that the song "Serenaded by Angels" by Kirk Talley was to be played. She heard that song sung by him so many years ago at a show at Dollywood in Pigeon Forge, Tennessee. She made dad buy her the cassette tape that day and she coined that as her funeral song. My Momma was truly serenaded by angels because she truly was one herself. She was my angel, my best friend, my strength and my go-to person for all my bad days. How was I going to live without her?

She never judged my emotional issues and she knew the depth of my struggles. She listened without judgment, she comforted without restraint and loved without limits. No one would ever be able to replace who she was to me. I didn't know how to carry on without her and how could we be planning this funeral for my Mom.

Walking into that room and seeing that beautiful rose-pink colored casket and my Momma laying there was a sight that was incomprehensible and nothing that you can be prepared to see. Momma looked beautiful that day because her best friend did her hair and makeup and made sure that she looked like herself and she even colored Momma's hair to remove the little bit of grey. Her makeup and lipstick were perfectly in place as always and she looked peaceful at that moment, but I was far from it.

So many things are a blur to me because I was in a state of emotional paralysis, but I do remember the visitation. So many people came in and out and gave words of love and hope, shared memories and paid their respects. Words of prayer and encouragement were given with the best of intentions by saying things like, "Mom wasn't suffering anymore" and that "we should have hope and peace because we will see her again pain and illness free." They would say the same thing over and over like, "You wouldn't want her back here like she was suffering," and others would say, "She is in a better place." I understood what they were saying, yet I was screaming inside "SHUT UP! I DO WANT HER BACK. NO MATTER WHAT AND NO MATTER THE CONDITIONS! I JUST WANT MY MOMMA! I NEED HER AND I CAN'T DO THIS WITHOUT HER!"

I had some friends from a previous job that came to the visitation. They brought me a beautiful and unique heart decoration made from a variety of buttons with different shapes and colors. They didn't say much to me verbally at that moment, but they just sat with me on the couch at the funeral home with their arms on my back and wrapped around my shoulders. No profound words of wisdom were spoken; however, their presence and support spoke volumes to me at that very moment. That was all I really needed and wanted at that time was to be seen and held. I didn't need advice or encouragement on how to cope or see things in a better or more Christian way. I needed to not feel all alone and I needed a friend. Yet I was surrounded by tons of people, but a dark cloud of loneliness was on me because my Mom, my best friend, was now gone forever.

I remember getting dressed for the funeral and wishing this was all a huge nightmare and that surely Momma wouldn't leave me or us. Her reputation was known for doing so many amazing things for the Lord,

His church and our family and had so much talent still to offer. She was one of the good ones and bad things aren't supposed to happen to them, Right?

The funeral was pretty much a daze going thru the process and only remembering tidbits of things here and there, but I do remember my Dad getting up and speaking during the services. He showed such strength and courage expressing beautiful sentiments about how Momma loved so many and how she shared that love with everyone whether a complete stranger or longtime friend. In my heart of hearts, I wanted to have that kind of strength and courage that he had, but my deepest desire was to just have my Momma back. When Dad finished speaking, he opened up the opportunity for anyone else to speak if they wanted to, but I chose not to. I couldn't muster up the strength nor the stamina to stand in front of the crowd and give a false impression to others that I was coping well and that I was doing okay because I wasn't. I felt that if I had chosen to speak at that moment it would have been a train wreck and I would have expressed what was really on my heart and mind which would not have been appropriate for celebrating the life of my mom when I was certainly not in a celebratory mood.

But if anyone knows our Wilkes family close enough, then they know that we are going to find something to laugh about during the worst nightmare of our lives. All the grandchildren rode together in one of the limousines to the cemetery and were excited to ride in a fancy car for the very first time. They didn't care, for those few moments, the reason why they were given the opportunity as they laughed and had a good time. It certainly helped lighten the mood on the drive to the cemetery as we traveled the few miles to lay my Momma to rest.

After all the services were over, the lunch was eaten, things were wrapped up, many tears were shed, necks were hugged, and final goodbyes were given, the time had come for me to return back home in Texas. I had to try and figure out living without my Momma. I felt as if I was a volcano boiling and bubbling with red molten lava waiting to erupt during the entire funeral process with all my true emotions and feelings. I was trying to keep them suppressed and in check, but I was wearisome holding back from spewing my anger, frustration, and fear. I was angry because my momma died way too early and that she was taken from me, my boys, our family and so many that she loved. My frustration was brewing towards everyone that was saying all these "consolable" expressions of comfort that I did not want to hear about her being in a better place and not suffering. But most of all, and the heaviest weight to bear was my fear of never learning how to live my life without her.

These were the thoughts that I contemplated over and over like a broken record repeating the same lyrics. Who was I going to call with parenting questions? Who was going to burn up the highways to always be there for support and every need or occasion in my life and my boys? Whose ear was going to listen to me when I was upset at Jason and needed someone to vent to and calm me down and tell me to pray? Who was going to really understand the depth of my anxiety and depression? Who was going to keep me from going off the deep end and allowing my emotions to completely rule me?

As these fears and worries escalated, I could feel myself spiraling downward internally, but it's not something of which you stop and take a personal evaluation. As a Christian, I knew the truth about having peace that my Momma was in Heaven. I knew that should be the overwhelming emotion in my heart, but it was polar opposite from what I was really experiencing. I felt my position as a preacher's wife, Mom, and leader didn't allow for me to lose control, show weakness, or crumble in grief so I just wore my "put together" masquerade and began living my new normal without her. But suppressing all the grief under the smiling mask only intensified the sporadic emotions, prolonged the grief, and damaged the relationships inside of my home and I had no idea how dangerous wearing that mask could be.

# 6

## Not Hiding from Everyone

A little child looks through the glass of a toy store with their nose pressed up against the window gazing at the toys, wishing and hoping that they could walk through the doors to the magical treasures of wishes and dreams inside, but somehow just can't seem to find where to enter the store as their frustration and desire continues to build. I was much the same way looking at consistency and peace within and without my own heart and mind. I looked through the glass as if everyone else was living what I considered normal and happy and wanted it so desperately. I just couldn't figure out how to enter that world myself.

As the days rolled by and life carried on, my depression and anxiety kept building. My visits to the doctor became more frequent and I kept trying to find something magical, perfect, and instant. I craved mending the deep pit of unhappiness, grief, and fear, that I was now experiencing, even more, because of my mom's death. It added a deeper layer altogether to my issues. I wasn't getting the answers I wanted to hear or the results from the medicines that I felt like I should be experiencing. My counselor just kept confirming that I was doing as good as could be expected with the grief that I had been through and that it was all a process. I was impatient and trying to control all of my road to peace because I wanted relief instantly.

From the way things looked from the outside, I was coping well with life considering the loss I just experienced from losing a loved one. I continued wearing a smiling masquerade appearing to have it all under control and surviving most days. There were many days when I was just too weary from putting on that facade all the time and I would fall to pieces. The fits of anger and rage would spew in our home, and I continued to blame and attack all those closest to me especially my husband.

Jason would be a buffer in our home between me and the boys when those days would occur. I would go on a frenzy through the house creating tons of damage not only in household items but in damaging words and demeaning attacks and then be overcome with guilt afterward. The rages felt as if they were out of body, and many times I would not even remember or realize what I was doing or what was being said. All of my energy was spent on the emotions and the outbursts and the pinned-up feelings would be released like a caged animal finally being set free.

Anyone that has lost a loved one knows that the first year is the hardest. It is experiencing everything for the first time without that person. I would blame the freshness of the sting of my Mom's passing as a validation for my actions and excuse my reactions as appropriate behavior of someone grieving. I would just claim that I was bipolar, and no one understood me. I would lash out and say that I was grieving and that I had lost my mother, excusing any and all my actions or reactions. All were acceptable in my eyes considering the circumstances.

The medicine list continued to grow longer and more extensive as I continued going to each doctor visit convincing them that things were not improving, but rather declining. There were so many prescriptions at this point and the cost to fill them monthly definitely exceeded a preacher's salary. I had to learn how to be resourceful to be able to afford everything. I would find creative ways with coupons to get whatever medicines I needed no matter the cost. None of the medicines were getting the job done, so we had to keep searching. I would contact drug manufacturers and get on patient assistance programs to help get medicines for free because it would not even be an option to consider, that I could or would be able to function without them. Desperate times called for desperate measures. At this point, Jason would do anything to try and make me happy and to keep peace in our home.

Visits back to my hometown now consisted of seeing my Dad and going to visit the cemetery. I would sit on the concrete bench, placed by another family, but was close to mom's gravesite, and just stare. I would glare at the granite headstone with my Mother's name on it and think to myself, why? The same thoughts would play over and over like a spinning merry go round and I couldn't find the way to jump off even though the thoughts were making me sick. Why did she have to be the one to go so early and how was I going to make it in life without her? I just couldn't get the thoughts to settle down in my mind nor in my heart.

The first Mother's Day was only a few months after mom's passing and it was a dreadful day for me. I was the one responsible to get the presents for the youth group to present to the Mother's on Sunday morning at church and that year I didn't even feel like celebrating. I really wanted to stay in bed and sleep the day away. It took every ounce of strength and energy for me to go to church services that day. Lifelessly, I mustered enough strength to go and compose myself. I tried to smile and wish other moms a warm welcome and greeting, but it was forced and not genuine. My boys were all excited to celebrate this day for me, so I painted on my lipstick smile. I smiled, fighting back the tears, and just pretended that it was a happy Mother's Day, but nothing could have been further from the truth.

The masquerade of the happy all together preacher's wife and mom were securely in place as I walked through the doors of the church that morning. I sat down after a few exchanges and greetings and then the song service began. I tried holding back the tears, but they began streaming down my face uncontrollably. The more I tried to hold them back the more powerful the floodgates opened. I erupted into sobs and quickly walked out the back door. A sweet friend followed me out. I just told her to tell Jason that I was okay, but I just couldn't handle it today. Not today! I went home.

The self-control and fortitude that was required to hold all my emotions together in public and hidden from everyone were beginning to weaken. I was convinced that none of the medications were working at this point. My dark days were getting darker and my energy level was depleted and life itself was quickly seeping out of me. The ability to remain in control and to hide the panic even in the slightest circumstances at home was gone. My emotions were even more chaotic and unpredictable. I kept searching for a cure for my broken heart, and for something to make me whole again. I was screaming silently for the constant turmoil to stop and the out of control downward spiral to cease.

All normal daily activities had become a chore. Going places that were unfamiliar and out of my comfort zone was a huge undertaking. Most environments and crowds outside of our own church setting were fearful to me. Fear was consuming me. Security for me had always been in the ability to be in complete control of my surroundings. Crowds simply did not permit that luxury due to all the elements and variables.

My sister and I had been going to a women's conference for many years. This particular year was to be no exception. I knew the venue for the conference had numerous steep steps, and for some reason, steps had become a trigger of fear for me. I was terrified that I would trip and go tumbling down, making a huge fool of myself. Each step became a tedious process as if I was climbing Mt. Everest. By the time I finally made it to the top, my breathing was extremely heavy, and it wasn't just because I was out of shape. The anxiety had escalated during the ascent!

I did tons of self-talking all the way into the building in a drastic effort to avoid a full-blown panic attack before reaching my reserved seat. I made it through the entire event and really enjoyed myself, forgetting the previous experience because I was distracted. But now the conference ended, and it was time to descend the stairs and return to the parking lot to go home. My short-term memory had started to become cluttered by all the medications, but I had not realized to what magnitude until I reached the front section of the parking lot. I walked out with the rest of the crowd as if everything was normal and my sister and I parted ways. But I was far from feeling normal, at this moment, as I walked around the busy parking lot looking for my vehicle.

I couldn't act like I was lost because I felt as if I would look stupid, so I just kept walking. My sister and her friends drove by laughing, not realizing at that point I was in a sheer panic not able to find my car. I called Jason in hysterics and panic because I truly was lost. I cried and yelled on the phone and then waited until the entire parking lot was bare so I could clearly spot my vehicle and I did.

I felt as if asking for help or telling someone that I was lost was a sign of weakness. Showing weakness required me to take off the masquerade of perfection, strength, and control. I could not allow myself to be seen by others as lost or scared. No matter the cost, or how many times I had to circle the parking lot that day looking for my vehicle or resorting to waiting until the parking lot was completely vacant, I would not cave.

May of 2009 Jason resigned from the church in Texas that he had been pastoring for 10 years and accepted a church in my hometown, back in Louisiana. Not only was it a church in my hometown but it was the church that I grew up in from the age of about four to the age of twenty-one. I felt as if this was going to be an ideal situation for me. Not that I was unhappy where we lived and the church that we were at, but that I would now be close to my family and surrounded by people that knew me as a little girl. I assumed that I could walk in the church and pick up where I had left off fourteen years ago. My struggles were completely foreign to them and my perception was that they would remember me as little Cindy. I hoped to be received as a little girl coming home and taken back in with open arms. I felt as if it was a clean slate and a fresh mask.

We packed everything up, the house, the boys, and the dog and moved across the state line, but as we all know, a life change requires adjustments. Finding new places to shop, a new hairstylist and new doctors is no easy undertaking. I was extremely excited about this change and felt as if I could now have new and fresh eyes on my files, medical history, and diagnosis. I was convinced that God would lead me to just the right doctor to "fix me." What I had not realized in all this process is that God was nowhere to be found. Not that He wasn't there because He is always waiting but that I was not seeking Him. I was not consulting him in anything. Yes, I prayed and "read" my Bible as any good Christian should, but it was all about going through the motions. As long as I kept doing things my way and in my own ability and keeping God at a distance, the cycle of depression and anxiety just continued while I was desiring to discover the perfect magic pill or combination of them to make my life perfect and happy.

I always did my homework checking on reviews of new doctors that I would consider seeing. Finding a new psychiatrist was on the top of my list of priorities when we relocated. The initial conversation with the office staff was my first indicator if the doctor was right for me. I required sincerity and true concern for my wellbeing by all those I would come in contact with because I was desperately on a journey to get well and they must understand that.

After the move, the first doctor that I chose to see was much older than what I was used to, and he had practiced neurology previously for many years. I had envisioned that this doctor would be knowledgeable about the mind and the emotions and had seen many different cases throughout the years. I was hopeful for my visit with him because of his experience, resume, and reviews.

My first visit began, as always, with the customary triage routine as I went through my list of medications with the nurse and explained how nothing was really working for me. I constantly talked trying to build a rapport with the personnel hoping that they would take me seriously and be considerate in the future. I divulged that I was still having very deep dark times and was constantly filled with anxiety. I then repeated much of the same information when I went back to see the doctor and talked with him face to face. I could tell by his demeanor and vocabulary that he was very smart but was also old school in his ways of diagnosing and treating mental illness. He talked to me about his personal preference in using older medications that were not used much anymore and explained how they were tried and true and that many doctors are more driven by the pharmaceutical companies by prescribing every new medication that comes out on the market. He believed that many younger doctors steered clear of the older medications that had been used in years past. He suggested that since I had tried many different other medications for mood stabilizing and was not seeing results that he would like to prescribe and recommend that I be put on Lithium.

I thought to myself, "Did I hear that correctly, Lithium?" I felt like I had heard of that medicine before in some old outdated books and movies. I was in shock because I believed that was prescribed for those that I considered "really psychotic" but was it really for me? He answered a lot of my questions that I had about it and was convinced that it was worth a shot trying it since it had not been prescribed to me yet and I had gone through so many other medications already. I trusted him because he was the doctor.

I had appointments once a month to check my weight, blood pressure, and my current state and frame of mind focusing on my level of depression and anxiety. Each visit the first thing that I did was weigh in. Each time I stepped on the old-fashioned scale, having metal weights to adjust the accurate reading when the needle stood still, more weights had to be moved towards the higher numbers because my weight continued to climb. In a period of about six months of taking the Lithium, I had gained back most of the weight I had lost since the lap band surgery.

When I would address my concerns and frustrations with the doctor about my increasing weight, he just kept excusing it as the medications adjusting in my body and that it would level off and come back down. His immediate concern was to get my mental state in proper balance. However, gaining all the weight back was causing my mindset to spiral downward even farther. I tried ignoring it and staying "in control" and hopeful, but things continued declining.

I could sense that it was getting harder and harder to be happy and to even fake it, so I decided to reach out to a Pastor friend of mine for counseling. I did believe deep down inside that the spiritual battles were parallel to my emotional and mental battles, but I didn't know how to cure it or how to even begin the process of healing. I always knew all the right answers; however, convincing myself to adhere to them and actually living them out was not quite as easy.

Wearing a mask day in and day out kept me protected. It was my privacy wall that kept me very guarded and secure. It was like putting RainX on my heart. When you apply RainX on your car, rain comes down and hits the windshield but doesn't stay. It immediately beads up and begins to roll off the glass. That is exactly how my heart transitioned into hiding from reality and the truth of who I was and who I was becoming. I believed in God and I knew in my heart that I was a born-again child of His. I also knew a lot of scriptures and could teach it to the little ones and the grown alike, but actually letting those scriptures that I was proclaiming to others to penetrate my own heart was not allowed. I just let it roll off like that RainX and kept my mask on with a smile while crumbling from within.

So, I wholeheartedly agreed with all the Biblically sound and practical advice that my new counselor was giving. He was a friend and local Pastor, and he was guiding with such honesty and love. I had every intention to always put all the suggestions that he offered into practice.

After meeting with him, I was excited and determined to get back to myself and to put into practice all the advice I was given, but I quickly fell into my old habits and my heart was very guarded and in denial. The Holy Spirit was drawing me into facing my true reality and not the one I had made up in my mind or the one that I lead others to see and believe. I knew all about Biblical healing of my heart and mind and grace to accept my failures and weaknesses, but I couldn't allow the reality of either to penetrate my heart and to pierce through the years of wearing the masquerade. Everything just kept rolling off. I had allowed my false identity and reality to take up residency in my life. Evidence of this is in my journal entry below. My heart knew deep down inside the struggles and the good intentions, but I didn't have the knowledge of how to stop being fake and applying truth in my own life and putting a halt to the person that everyone knew.

Here is March 2011.

> *You see, I was overcome with grief also. I had lost my Mom just a few years ago and I had never dealt with that. It was time. I remembered the nurse telling me a tactic to use that may help overcome grief. Write my Mom a letter and tell her everything I thought she needed to know. So, I did, I told her everything, my depression, my anger, and my resentment. I went to the graveside and I read the letter out loud so I could hear the words, then I burned it. I set it on fire, never to pick it up again. My grief was gone no longer to be shackled by it. I still miss her deeply and always will, but I can now go on and live my life and wait till the day I get to see her in Heaven.*
>
> *Now to deal with the anxiety and depression, I decided to go see a Christian counselor again. I began to learn that God allowing me to have this disease was not a punishment nor a curse (even though it felt like it). I was chosen for a reason because in His infinite wisdom He has a purpose for everything. He had a purpose for my life beyond the Bipolar.*
>
> *I was doing better with the anxiety. I still take 3 pills a day for it, but it is managed. I was having trouble in crowds*

*like staying in church, and the grocery stores and stuff, but even that has gotten better. I have come to realize that I am going to be alright and nothing is going to happen to me.*

*I started to deal with my Spiritual wall also. I had left God so many years ago and now I wanted and desired a deep personal relationship with Him again. I knew I was saved. As we Baptist call it, I was backslidden. I was way, way back. But all it took was, what I call a coming to Jesus meeting, and getting serious. First with my confession of sins, then a deep yearning and transparency with the Lord. I was assigned Bible readings by my counselor and we would discuss them. I was truly thirsting for Him and His word and that hadn't happened in years.*

*So, as you see, you can get past feeling like you've been cursed by God for your disease or ailment. Being a child of God is what makes us special, and He is calling for you to come home. So as my favorite artist Mandisa sings, "take the shackles off my feet, and I want to dance, I want to dance, take the shackles off my feet, I just want to praise you, I just want to praise you." Let that be your prayer to overcome the bondage of your disease. No, I am not cured, but I am beginning to learn how-to live-in God's will. I will continue to share my story.*

So along with the new move, I decided that working outside of the home and changing my daily scenery would be a beneficial thing. I was determined to find a job that brought me joy and gave me a feeling of purpose. Working with children was always a passion of mine and so I went and applied at daycare centers. I was hired at the first daycare that I had applied.

After just a few short weeks of working, I developed an overwhelming feeling that I was being sucked into an unorganized drama filled torture chamber. Not something this girl needed and not an environment that a control freak perfectionist could handle on an everyday basis. Chaos externally did not mix well with the already tornadic internal struggle that I was continually living with.

I quit my job without even giving a two weeks' notice. I informed them that I would finish out the week but would not be returning after that. Then after a few months of not being employed, I found another daycare that was labeled as "Christian." I had hope that this setting would be a more positive work environment and that it would be favorable to my needs with having a Christian atmosphere and employees surrounding me every day. This daycare was a great place to work and I enjoyed most aspects of it, but of course, I was the new employee and got stuck with the discipline problem classroom.

I liked to label myself as a strong disciplinarian both as a mother and a teacher. It sounds much better to say that than to admit controlling and obsessive-compulsive person needing structure. It was a way of relabeling my control issues as if they were a good attribute and denying the magnitude of how they consumed me. I liked order and always stuck to the rules. It was much easier to live with the "disciplinarian" disguise then admitting to myself that there was a deep-rooted problem.

I was proud of my classroom management and impeccable structure with lesson plans and teaching. Having order and not deviating from my plans gave me the satisfaction of controlling something. Order externally made it easier to lie to myself that I was struggling so bad internally. I stayed a little longer at this job than the previous one but decided to quit it too. I just couldn't maintain the persona of living "normal" while my emotions were chaotic. I had a deep desire to stay busy and make myself feel somewhat productive, so I decided to open a daycare in my home. I felt as if it was the perfect solution to be able to remain in my familiar environment, control all aspects of it, bring in some income, and still enjoy being with children.

I did that for about a year and a half on a part-time basis. As soon as the kids would go home, I would go to bed in exhaustion. The laundry got washed but then piled up. The migraines from stress got even worse so my church attendance became less, and I would find ailments and issues to keep me from having to do anything except what was absolutely necessary.

Jason and I struggled in our relationship. He continued walking around on eggshells most days waiting for my next explosion. I developed the habit of jumping in the car and going for a drive when things would get out of hand or my emotions were spiraling out of control. Sometimes it was just around the block and other times I would drive without a clear destination contemplating whether to go home or to never stop. I dreamed about the day when I would get in the car and just keep driving until I ran out of gas. When I stopped, that would be where I would start a new life.

I didn't care about going to a specific destination. I just wanted as far away as possible from the mess that I had made and the person that I had become. It was not my husband, my kids, my job, or even my church. It was me! I wanted to escape from myself. I wanted to run away from the person that I didn't recognize in the mirror anymore and the person that was destroying the hearts of those closest to her. I wanted a do-over but didn't know how. I was searching for a miracle and all the right answers with the best of intentions but in all the wrong places.

My husband tried over and over to make me happy, yet it was never good enough. He would often plan small trips for our anniversary to reconnect. His hope was that the change of scenery would allow me to relax. It did temporarily, but no matter where I went or how great the vacation was, I still couldn't escape from myself. I vividly remember one trip where we decided to go to Hot Springs, Arkansas. It was a great couple of days but the turmoil inside of me was too strong. I knew that I should be happy but wasn't. I knew I should be having fun but couldn't. I knew I should be thankful but was anything but that. It was getting harder and harder to fake the smile and pretend to be enjoying myself. I was sinking into a pit that was deep and dark and scary.

I remember taking a bath one evening after spending all day sightseeing and enjoying ourselves. Sitting there listening to the water coming out of the faucet and screaming at the top of my lungs inside my mind. Contemplating laying down in the water and holding my breath. I was thinking that it wouldn't take long to stop breathing, but I was too scared to do anything. No words could come out of my mouth to ask for help or to call out to Jason, just tons of self-harming thoughts bombarding me to end it all. I then transferred my attention to the razor on the edge of the bathtub. It was just sitting there glaring at me. My head was saying just pick it up and get it over with, but my heart was saying Cindy, you are too scared. You need help.

I focused on it waiting a few minutes, for what seemed like an eternity. I desired with every fiber inside of me for the feeling to go away. I wanted all the struggles to end. I wanted this life to be over. I just wanted to be me and free from all the messes that I had made and the person I had become. I wanted to scream for help but didn't know what to say or how to explain it, so I just got out of the bathtub and sat on the white, cold tile floor and wept. I cried out for Jason and he came in and found me balled up in the corner. I told him I was scared and everything that I was thinking even the dark, self-harming thoughts and he just held me. I fell limp in his arms and wanted to just melt away.

By that evening, I pulled myself back together and took my handful of medications before bed. I went along with the rest of the trip as if nothing had happened. I did not realize, at that time, the magnitude of what was happening as if those thoughts were somehow normal. That the constant fighting, the running away for several minutes and sometimes hours, was a normal occurrence in other homes, not realizing that it was not natural nor healthy. I could take off the masquerade at home and feel relief, but you better believe it was neatly positioned in place anytime I was out of the confines of that house. This journal entry was my mentality at this time always minimizing the toll that my actions were taking on my family.

> *Our Lord is such a gentleman that He doesn't force Himself on anyone. He patiently waits for you to come back to Him. He never moved. So that is where I am at, at His feet drawing from His gracious love and mercy.*
>
> *I still have my days where everything is not so "peachy" as we like to call it. I have been sick with a migraine for the past 3 days and had to get a shot for it. Days like this I struggle, I just want to feel better and have God take the pain away. Sometimes He does and sometimes He has us to wait awhile.*
>
> *One thing that I learned to do because I had felt like I had accomplished so many things in the past but wasn't moving forward now was make a list of goals. The Bible says, " where there is no vision the people will perish." So, I needed a vision for my life. Write 5 personal goals, 5 family*

goals, and 5 spiritual goals. This will help you work on things you want to accomplish in your life. It sets your mind on positive things so that you are not idle.

When I get idle, is when my depression creeps up. I began to dwell on things of the past. Why? I don't know. Those things are forgiven. Was Jesus' blood not good enough for me, for those things that I did? That I can't be forgiven for them? What I am basically saying, is that His sacrifice was not enough for my sins and I can't be forgiven. I know that not to be true so why dwell on the past? The Bible says, "look to the things that are before me." That is where my list comes into place. Read them daily to remind yourself of those goals that you have set for yourself.

Depression is an awful illness because it not only affects you but the people around you. It is usually the ones closest to us. I finally received help when I realized my boys where being affected by it. My husband was a grown man and he understood some of what I was going through, but my boys just knew Mommy was sick. I didn't want them growing up thinking Mommy was sick, so I got help. I still have those days of blues and that is ok, but I relish in the fact that it is not going to conquer me. I will have a better day tomorrow. I also don't beat myself up for it either. I just have my day where I sleep a little more or do a little less, but I always try to do a little something so I can feel good about that accomplishment.

I called this title becoming a worker bee because having bipolar and an anxiety disorder, is work. It is daily working on my mental state, attitude and walk with the Lord. Not that every day is perfect, but we can get to a point where the highs are not so high, and lows are not so low, and the changes are farther apart. Today slow down enough that you can see the fingerprints of the Lord in your life.

As the summer rolled around, it was now time for Church Camp. It was July of 2012, and I had not missed many church camps since I was six years old. It was the highlight of my summer getting to spend time isolated from the world in a cabin filled with girls drawing closer to the Lord. This particular year our church was assigned to bunk in the cabin with my sister in law's church. I was excited and knew it would be a blast spending the entire week together. The issue I had not thought through was the fact that church camp is scheduled with continuous activities back to back which did not allow for much rest or downtime. At home, I had gotten into the routine of resting every day and having tons of downtime each time I struggled. I would go to bed and sleep trying to escape from the world on a regular basis.

Being in a cabin full of girls, sleeping in a wooden bunk bed and staying busy from sun up to sun down was not settling well with me or my traditional routine. So, I slept. I slept a lot that week. I missed church services, didn't socialize with others like normal and isolated myself from most everyone. I excused and blamed my actions on the medicines and the "migraines." That response had become an easy go-to rationalization to give to others and to myself. I slept the entire week away. Friday rolled around as camp came to an end and it was time to go back home to my life. This journal entry explains how I was feeling at this time.

> *How is it that you can be surrounded by wonderful people and still feel alone? I often feel that way. My own insecurities get in the way. They are always whispering in my ear to keep me from being the true me. I know that is Satan's tactics to keep me down. But why do I listen to him and allow him to determine my mood or my mindset? I have listened to him so long that I believe him, that God's promises are foreign to me. I know what they say but do I believe them in my heart? It's that part of "renewing of your mind" that I have trouble with. I often put a mask on that everything is ok, not always but sometimes. Mostly in public where I am constantly looking over my shoulder wondering who is saying what. I deal with that mostly because of my weight. Why can't I just take the mask off or why can't I be secure in who I am? I know I can in Christ but knowing and doing is a much harder task. My prayer is that I can just be me.*

*That I can be me in a crowd and stand tall and proud of who I am and who God has made me. That I can stop wearing masks and let people know what is truly going on inside so they can pray for me. I pray that others, as well as myself, will listen to the one true voice and not those negative voices of Satan keeping us defeated.*

On a lazy Saturday, a month or two after church camp, to my surprise the doorbell rang at home out of nowhere. We weren't expecting any guests to my knowledge. The last people I expected to be at my front door were my brother and sister. He didn't live too far from me, but she lived about three hours away. They had popped in for a surprise visit, wanting to express face to face their deep concern for me and the shape that I was in.

I sat down in the recliner and just listened. I was quiet and subdued for a few moments, feeling the warmth creeping up my neck and into my face, a natural response for me when I was nervous, anxious, or mad. My anger began bubbling up inside waiting to explode. I was defensive, hurt, and downright irate at their words. How could they judge me? They expressed their concern that I had lost myself, was too heavily medicated and acted like a zombie. At that moment, I felt betrayed by my own family. To say that I was furious was an understatement! I was appalled that they felt like they had the right to advise me on how I was doing as if they knew more than my doctors. I informed them with anger and tears, hurt and betrayal weighing so heavy on my heart, that they needed to walk in my shoes and see what it felt like to live with bipolar. I felt like when they could do that then they could diagnose me and tell me what medicines to take and not take but until then leave me alone. I now know that my sister and brother were attempting to hold an intervention type meeting on me that day, but it didn't work. They left with me feeling even more alienated and alone and very angry.

I was so angry that I was determined to prove to them that I needed each and every one of the prescribed medications that I was taking and if they, not being my doctors, felt that I was taking too much or didn't need them all, then fine I will show them. I will just stop my medicines and see what happens and how bad things really can get. I did just that by stopping one here and taking less there while moods started becoming more and more sporadic and unpredictable in a very short time. I repeated to myself and to my husband over and over in response to their visit, "They think I am crazy taking all these drugs then let's just prove how crazy I can get not taking them."

I justified every single action I did, validated every single diagnosis that I had been given and lived out every single symptom or reaction that I read about in the medical dictionary for a person with my diagnosis. I lived out having bipolar to its fullest potential and I took every medication prescribed to me as directed. Our bathroom counter looked like a pharmacy littered with little brown bottles with white caps and I learned to swallow a handful at a time because I was taking so many. Taking one at a time would have taken forever with the number of medications that I was on at the time.

My sister and brother were right, and I really had become a shell of a person, but I just couldn't see it. The mask was still intact to the outside world, but I was in denial that some were starting to see a few small cracks or tattered spots in it. I tried to carefully maintain the persona that I had created and kept playing the part. I had even convinced myself that I was who I was and the person that I had been portraying to others. I believed that there wasn't an issue, I was in denial that I had created a body double type facade to maintain my coverup. I was convinced that I couldn't control myself. My personal image of myself was so distorted. I truly believed my actions were not detrimental to anyone but myself. My view of reality, of who I had become, and the effects that it was having on my family, was completely selfish and self-satisfying to not make me directly accountable for anything. All the while I was being able to blame my mental health diagnosis and the medications.

So, most days were filled with anger projecting my unhappiness onto everyone else because I felt as if I couldn't be truthful with anyone about what was really going on. I felt if others knew my deep, ugly secrets it would cause them to doubt everything I created myself to be, the validity of the words I spoke and potentially hurt our family and my husband's ministry. Small doubts and thoughts would enter my mind causing me to reflect on what my sister and brother had said to and about me. I would think, "What if I really was just fooling myself?" But I felt the fear of someone finding out the truth about my secret life was a bigger burden to carry. Did I really have a problem? Was I really a zombie? Who had I become? Was any of this truly not normal? Was I bipolar? Why won't God take this all away?

Once again even deeper depression set in as I tried to figure everything out and ponder the million doubts and thoughts racing through my mind each moment. It was as if the sunshine was trying to find a crack in the clouds somewhere, but the storm had rolled in and dark clouds just seemed to stay. The anxiety piled on and my good days became fewer and the bad days- well that was almost every day. I put on a good smile to keep my babies at my in-home daycare or to attend church. I could always muster up the energy to do a good job at both places, but the minute they went home, or I left the building, I would go back to bed or the anger and rage would start again and again and again. It was if I was playing the roles of Dr. Jekyll and Mr. Hyde. One moment completely controlled and then the switch would flip, and the pent-up emotions would burst and come out. I was in control enough to know that I couldn't stop "normal" activity because that would have been a tell-tale sign that something was truly wrong. No one could know what went on behind the closed doors of that parsonage or in the depths of my sick heart.

One night, the weight I was carrying was too much to bear and the guilt and anxiety were like a weight of bricks crashing down and crushing my heart. No matter what I tried to do the fear of never being normal, getting real help, or finding peace was intensifying. The deep dark thoughts of life and my family being better off without me started to creep in again. I never had an action plan to actually end my life, but Satan was planting those self-deprecating thoughts and ideas of hurting myself in my head again. I felt as if I was too much of a burden and was placing too much on my family. This night the darkness got darker and the thoughts were beginning to scare me. I knew I needed help and told Jason about my fear and so he made a phone call to the hospital and talked to a nurse which happened to be an old friend that worked there. She advised him that I needed to be brought to the hospital, so off we went.

We were instructed by the nurse friend to go through the emergency room at Willis Knighton Hospital North which had a psychiatric ward. Most of the preliminary check-in details are a blur, but I do remember all the negative thoughts continually running through my head. The constant thinking the same destructive things over and over reminded me of an old film projector that had finished, and the film reel just keeps spinning while the film hits the projector over and over making an annoying banging noise until someone turns off the machine. The thoughts were spinning over and over in my mind and I couldn't make them stop. I just needed someone to turn them off because I couldn't do it myself.

That night I was admitted in the psychiatric ward for the first time. I told Jason goodbye and I was rolled in a wheelchair to the elevator while being escorted by a police officer. I knew this had to be serious to need security just to go to the other floor. The nurses checked me in and explained that they had to keep my bags in order to search them. I also had to be searched and checked from head to toe. The only thing they allowed me to keep that night was a family picture of Jason and my boys.

I was escorted into my room which was the 24-hour suicide watch room. The room was bare with just a bed and a sheet, no pillow or blanket. I was instructed that the doors remained open and the lights on. There was one bathroom in the room, but no door was on that either. I knew the moment that I walked into that room things just got seriously real. It was like scenes from a movie and something that others go through or experience. I felt this wasn't the type of place for this preacher's wife. This could not be my reality. I believed a psychiatric ward was for people who were in really bad shape, not for people like me that just had some emotional problems. I was convinced that I only needed a doctor to find the right medicine or combination of medicines and I maintained that stance during my stay. That was my focus that I was consumed with at that time.

I cried and tried to pray a lot that night. As you can see from this writing in my journal immediately after my stay in the hospital that I knew where to turn and I had the best of intentions but knowing and applying are completely different concepts.

> *That has been my answer to it all...run away from everything and never look back. When I run out of gas and money,*

that is where I will be. Never realizing my issues would go with me. I missed out on so much of life and activities with my family and my relationship with the Lord was practically non-existent. He never moved but I felt as if I couldn't pray anymore and didn't get anything from reading my Bible. That happens when you allow Satan to have rule and reign over your thoughts for so many years.

Then one day I snapped and I grabbed the razor and I was going to finally end it all and go be with my Momma and my husband walked in. He immediately realized what was going on and said get dressed you are going to the Hospital. Well, I thought, "great, now I can get away from it all." Sadly, was I mistaken. We went and they committed me for major depression with suicidal thoughts. I thought I would stay a few days sleep all day and get my much-needed vacation. Oh, I was so wrong. As I was escorted in a wheelchair up to the floor, a policeman had to go with me. Then I realized this must be serious. Then they began processing me and checking my things in. They searched me and took away everything but the clothes on my back and a picture of my family.

I was placed in the observation room for the night. It was the scariest place in the world to me. I hated being so alone in a room with someone coming in every so often checking on me. I finally cried and I cried out to the Lord for help and strength. I needed Him. Why is it that we must get so down and deep into a situation before we cry out to God for help? If something was happening to my children and they called for me I would immediately come running. Well, that is what I did. I cried out to Jesus, but he didn't have to come running. He was already there. I just didn't realize it.

I didn't sleep much that first night as I just kept thinking about what people were going to think. What will they say about Cindy Hebert being in a psychiatric ward? See I have always been concerned and consumed with what others were thinking about me instead of thinking about myself and what was in my best interest. That is why wearing a masquerade was such a necessity for me. If I didn't wear it then people would find out what was really hidden underneath my smile. At this moment in this place, I couldn't hide anymore! My brokenness was real!

I cried and prayed most of the night clinging to my picture of my husband and our boys. Hoping that this nightmare would end soon but knowing that I wasn't asleep because I really couldn't get any with the fluorescent lights shining on me the entire evening. I survived the evening, and the next morning I was moved into a semi-private room and was comforted that I had a nice roommate. We immediately began talking about the fact that she had been in the hospital for some time and so she gave me the rundown on how things operated. It was time for breakfast, and I walked down to the cafeteria area still wearing the same clothes that I entered the hospital in and got in line for my medications before I ate. The nurse informed me that the doctor on call had made a few adjustments to my prescriptions. I was hopeful at that moment because I was convinced that the medicines I had been taking were not helping and that was originally why I was in there anyway.

I sat quietly at the table eating and really observing everyone as they came in. People were very raw and honest at the breakfast table with why they were in the hospital and the struggles that they were facing. Yet when I was asked, I just answered with the simple phrase that "I needed some medicine adjustments." I never could open up to admit the depth of my issues. I wouldn't give a voice or speak out loud about the suicidal thoughts that I had just a few short hours before or about the fact that if I had money for a plane ticket or a new life that I would jump at the chance to do it. I didn't know how to admit to myself or much less anyone else that I couldn't function without taking a handful of drugs every day. I was in denial that I hated myself, my life, and was just existing, as I continued to hide behind the smile even at the table that morning.

I was carefully observing, studying the body language, and analyzing each conversation. I was building myself up in my head and believing that I was completely different than those people sitting around me. I was proclaiming to myself, "I am not like them. I am not that messed up. I am not that bad off." Internally, I kept validating that things were not that bad with me and I was certainly on a different level than all the others. The fact that I had a job, I was a preacher's wife and my kids were thriving was my rebuttal to the fact that I was in a psychiatric ward. I was convinced that I just had a few issues and just needed a little help with some coping skills and a break from my stressors. I was in complete denial, not realizing the magnitude of where I was and why I was there.

I started getting completely overwhelmed at breakfast and could feel the red whelps and flush face coming over me as I was sitting there contemplating why I was even there. I decided to remove myself from the situation instead of sitting there exposing myself and my weaknesses. As I walked down the hall, I remember my legs getting heavier and my arms felt as if they were dragging the floor. My roommate had already told me the key to getting out of the hospital quicker was to participate in everything that was offered. At that moment, I just wanted to melt into the concrete floors because I couldn't go on. I finally got to the end of my hall and hurled myself into the bed with the last bit of energy I had. I just laid there and cried and wept all over again. Then the anxiety and panic came over me. I was all alone. My husband and boys were not there with me. Then the thoughts about the truth being found out consumed me. I kept thinking about what Jason was telling people about where I was and why I wasn't doing my normal daily activities.

Just as my breathing got more labored and my heart began to race, the morning nurse came into my room. She came to my bedside and asked if I was ok. I couldn't speak. I was numb. My breathing was so labored at that point it was as if I had just run an Olympic race in record time. I could feel the heat penetrating off my face and the redness was as if I had been in the hot sun laying on a beach for hours feeling the results of a sunburn. My eyes just glanced over at her and all I could do was shake my head no. That was my very first acknowledgment that I was not alright to anyone and even to myself.

This elderly nurse softly and tenderly started speaking to me. Her soft yet chubby manicured hands with light pink fingernail polish grabbed my right hand. She began to rub my hand ever so gently as if she was petting a brand-new puppy for the first time. She began to talk in a tone that you often hear on relaxation and meditation recordings. She started explaining that my feelings, at that moment, were not real. She began teaching me how to cope during a panic attack.

Slowly she went through each of the five senses naming them one by one, causing me to understand their reality. She emphasized concentrating on facts, and that panicking, and anxiety was not real. Beginning with the sense of touch, that dear nurse explained that the touch of her hand on my arm was real. She then asked me to open my eyes and to look at her. Although my eyes were stinging from profuse tears, and I was consumed with the fear of what was taking place, I opened them anyway. She asked me to look at her, to understand that she was real, and then look around the room. She asked if I could see anything on the wall, and of course, I replied with a "yes!" I could see the clock and the calendar. She affirmed that the sense of sight was reality. She continued on to the sense of smell, asking if I could still smell the breakfast aroma lingering down the hall. I acknowledged the smell of bacon lingering through the hospital floor. She explained how the smell was also real. The sense of hearing was explored and acknowledged by the ticking of the clock as the second hand revolves from one number to the next. It was a faint sound but as I began intentionally listening, it was real nonetheless. Finally, she asked me if I could taste anything. I did, the saltiness from the tears that had streamed down my face earlier. That too was real.

During the entire process of the reality of my own five senses, the nurse encouraged me to take a deep breath in between each and every response. My breathing and pulse began to resume to normal. The panic attack was over. I no longer felt myself vanishing into the mattress of the hard hospital bed. It was over. The nurse nonchalantly stated that any time I felt a panic attack coming on, I only had to follow the steps of the "real senses." That I needed to stop myself and realize what is truly real in my presence. The things, thoughts, and worries that were consuming me and causing me to become anxious and panic were not real. The worries of what-ifs and whys were simply formulated in my head.

The nurse who comforted me had been a complete reminder of my own momma. I don't know if it was her soft, chubby hands, her tone that she talked to me or just her loving nature, but I look back now and realize that God took care of me even when I felt as if my world was crashing in on me. While I was doubting my own existence or the reason that I was still alive, God knew who I needed and sent her into my room that day. The amazing thing is that she exposed me to something as simple as the five senses, something I could do by myself, at any time or any place when anxiety began to creep in.

So, after I finally pulled myself back together, I took a shower and wandered down the hall to attend my first group therapy. After group therapy, I met with the psychiatrist. State law mandates anyone that has been admitted to the psychiatric ward to have a psychiatrist check within 72 hours. I explained to him my depression and anxiety issues downplaying the severity and trying to convince him that things were not as bad as they seemed. I had an excuse for my actions and told him that I just was in a rough season of my life and that I was already feeling better. I had become a great manipulator with all the right words to say after the walls of destruction tumbled down and my heart was depleted of all emotions. I would dismiss it all away making light of the situation and putting on my best masquerade as if this was just a onetime occurrence.

I could not admit to myself that the continual outbursts even occurred, and I would downplay the fact that I desperately needed help. The bottom of the pit was where I had taken up residence. I had gotten comfortable down there and the destructive self-harming thoughts were beginning to come more often than not. But I knew, oh so well, how to put on my "having it all together pretty mask" and convince myself and everyone else that it really wasn't that bad. I was confident that I could convince the doctors of the same, and I did.

I ended up staying in the hospital for five days as my medicine was adjusted and stabilized. I became very comfortable and friendly with my roommate who was an alcoholic. She was a beautician, so of course, we had similar interests. I also remember that my neighbors were two brothers that suffered from schizophrenia. They would often wander into our room with funny hallucinations and make us laugh. They would say things that were completely unrealistic and act in what I considered a very less than the normal way. Not making light of their disease and struggles, I would justify my actions by comparing myself to those brothers. I would put myself and my actions up on a pedestal comparing the level of my "normal" behavior and being in touch with reality. I rationalized and defended my behavior and scrutinized their actions. Yet, both of us were suffering with reality.

I don't recall too many of the other details from my hospital stay other than a serious medicine change up with my new psychiatrist. Some of my family did come to visit me, one of them being my dad. When he entered the room, I remember hugging him as if I was a little girl all over again. Inside I was screaming for him to help his baby girl, but all the while trying to maintain my composure appearing to once again have things in complete control. My husband also came for several visits and attended the family sessions with me.

One of the therapists explained that the things that are taught to us while in the hospital and in therapy sessions may not be applicable to our present situations, but we needed to file it away for future use as if they were tools in our toolbox. Those tools consisted of tactics, knowledge, and strategies for coping and managing life and they were available to be used when the need arose. We were educated in several different sessions, by different therapists and coaches, regarding the fact that medicine could only do so much and that it was just one of those tools to aid our functioning. We were informed that we needed to do the work ourselves to achieve recovery and that medicine was just to accompany our actions to be able to be a healthy functioning member in society.

But, you see, I didn't see myself as a non-functioning member in society. I only saw myself as having just a few coping issues. I felt as if everyone could use a few behavior adjustments if they had to deal with the amount of stress that was placed on me being a mom, wife, preacher's wife, and also having lost my best friend, my mom. I felt completely fine and safe inside the confines of the hospital and I found it so easy having no real pressures of daily tasks. The most effort I had to put forward was just getting myself dressed and walking down to the cafeteria, day room or to group therapy. That didn't take too much effort so the weight of all my burdens was lightened for those few days. In all reality, my hospital stay only further skewed my perception of myself believing that I was not that bad off and that I didn't have any real problems compared to others that I encountered in there. The masquerade I was wearing had deceived my own heart and wouldn't allow reality to penetrate.

After being released from the hospital, I was welcomed home by a clean house, the mountain of laundry put away and everything neatly in order. Remember, the housework and laundry had gone by the wayside and my husband had been too overwhelmed, as any man would be, caring for two young sons and dealing with a sick wife. He had taken up all the slack being both the mom and dad, getting them where they needed to be, pastoring a church and living with my unpredictable behavior. During my hospital stay, my family members came to our home and cleaned for us, completely overhauling it. They wanted me to arrive home with a fresh start, not be overwhelmed with the daunting task of getting things back in order.

At first, I was a little taken back because I had been in complete denial of the condition of our home, but Jason excitedly described all that had been accomplished. Mounds of clean clothes that had been thrown on our bedroom floor for weeks had been freshly laundered. We had gotten to the point where we would just dig thru them time and time again to try and find that much-desired article of clothing or the pair of socks that actually matched. Thank goodness that matching socks were not really on the high priority list of my boys during that time.

I stepped back for a moment and realized how nice this fresh clean house was, I was thankful. Thankful for a split moment. But my happiness didn't last. It was very short lived. When I went into the kitchen that evening to get something out of a cabinet and realized some of my cabinets had been rearranged, I was livid that someone questioned my ability to choose the proper placement of my dishes. Once again, the war began.

The angry and frustrated words started flying out of my mouth like poisonous venom spewing towards anyone close by. I conveyed that no one was considering my feelings or what I was going through. I once again took the victim role and justified my actions by telling myself that no one had the right to come in and move my kitchen around. I believed it was crossing the line and an invasion of my personal space. Everything was always all about me and how no one ever considered my feelings and my struggles.

I was selfish, and in self-preservation mode, not regarding the toll that it was taking on my husband and my family because I was staying guarded. I would not allow myself to truly open up my heart to any therapist or doctor and would certainly never tell the complete truth. I would downplay the severity of my struggles and remained discreet to the point that it appeared I was still completely in control except for having a few minor issues.

My actions could be described as a treacherous thunderstorm with tornadic activity with only an umbrella for a mask. I remained outside during the storm's calamity feeling just fine all by myself because I have the umbrella in my hand. I never realized that I wasn't the only one braving the storm. My husband and our two sons were weathering the same tornado right along with me. My arms were tiring, and the wind was brutal against me as I clung the umbrella tightly. The tattered umbrella was now wavering, flopping and flying with each gust of wind. The sheets of rain drenching my hair and clothing. Yet, I stubbornly and proudly refuse to drop the umbrella and just go indoors where it was safe. There was such a need to remain in full control, and I had to be the one to hold the umbrella, as a warrior, sacrificing my own sanity.

What I didn't take into account was the amount of energy it took to remain steadfast against the storm hailing down on me. It was taking a toll on me. My arm muscles began to ache and quivered with the passing of time, but I was too stubborn. I refused to give up control. Even though those precious little eyes of my boys were looking up at me. They spoke volumes without uttering a word. Those eyes were saying, "Momma, it's going to be ok, let's just go," but I wouldn't budge or move. Taking down the umbrella and going inside would mean I had failed and was giving up. It would mean, to me, that I was not able to take care of everything by myself. It would mean that I failed and that I was not strong enough. It would require admitting that I was weak. I had not realized the rain was now showering down on me while drenching my husband and my kids. We were all soaking wet, tired and freezing cold. The elements had taken a toll on all of us, yet, I stood there still holding on to the umbrella as the masquerade continued.

If I only I could grasp the concept of the promise given in scripture that states, "when I am weak then I am strong." (2 Corinthians 12:10) It would have been so much easier to stop wrestling myself and to claim the promise, "Come to me all ye who are weary and heavy laden, and I will give rest." (Matthew 11:38) The issue all rested on the fact and the foundational truth that I couldn't bring myself to the point of even admitting was that I was weak and/or weary. Not being able to confess that I couldn't do it by myself and that I didn't have it all figured out and together made me completely blinded to that fact I needed Jesus. I was in denial that I even needed help. I felt I had no need for Jesus to make me stronger or to take my burden. He was in my heart but nicely placed on a shelf for display not an actual integral part of my life.

I still believed that I was doing just fine holding it all together with my masquerade neatly in place and the smile plastered on my face, my hair neatly styled and my clothes and jewelry in impeccable shape. Inwardly my heart was tattered and torn just like that umbrella and so was the relationship with my family. We were all drenched from the storms of life and our love was waxing cold, but I just kept smiling behind my mask, oblivious to reality.

I tried keeping up the persona and maintaining the pace of normalcy, but the marathon of perfection and strength was making me very weary. After leaving the hospital, I had to find a new doctor. Doctor visit after doctor visit came and went; however, my unstable emotions caused me to go from the usual once per month checkups to now being every other week. At my new doctor, I would appear to be stable and on top of the world during the visit then I would call the doctor back within a week and inform her that I had plummeted down once again. The doctor would call me back and ask what was causing such drastic changes between each visit and I never could explain or pinpoint the cause. I would make urgent phone calls to her as if my house was burning down because I was desperate to find some relief and peace and that I felt as if nothing was working. My deepest desire was to keep searching for something to fix me, but nothing was able to, because I was in self-denial and couldn't be truly honest with myself or my doctor.

I had built a good relationship with my doctor and had gained her trust. I went so often that she was now not requiring me to actually go into the office to see her every time I was in a "crisis" moment. I could call her, and we would discuss things over the phone, or I could send an email. If she felt that it was necessary at the moment, she would advise me to tweak the dosage of my medications, whether up or down, or switch some of them altogether. My list of medications by this point had become very long and extensive.

I routinely swallowed pill after pill each and every morning as it was my checklist of daily to do's and duties. Then watching the clock during the day, as if my life depended on it, I waited for the hands to reach 2:00 pm so that I could take my afternoon benzodiazepine medicine. It was like dangling a piece of meat in front of a pack of starving wolves sometimes pacing, waiting, and anticipating swallowing that afternoon pill. Then bedtime would roll around and the handfuls of drugs would be swallowed once again.

For the life of me, I could not comprehend why I was still having so many issues. I would sleep all the time not knowing if I was truly depressed or just blaming it on the medicines. It was probably a little of both or just the fact that I wanted to escape from life. I continued to have viscous outbursts in our home and just blame it on stress, the bipolar, or the medicines. I always had a logical explanation and reason behind every action or reaction that I had. After these outbursts, I would always feel completely guilty but in the middle of them, I had no clue what was happening. My temper would flare, my emotions would run high and my mouth would discharge cruel and hurtful things. Many times, even some not so appropriate colorful words would be said.

I would lose control of myself and the more Jason would try to reason with me the more exuberant the fit became. I would reach such a high level of frustration at times that I would resort to pulling my hair and hitting myself in the head with my hand. I would call myself stupid and crazy over and over. I was trying to get a reaction, deflect the pain and take the pressure off of myself and onto what I would blame as the disease and everyone else for not understanding.

My anxiety and fears had reached an all-time high and driving was just too overwhelming, so I quit driving for a period of about six months. I also could not handle any environment that I was not directly in control of and I did not leave my house during that six-month period except to go to church which was considered my safe zone. I did not do any of shopping and had even stopped all my Dollar General runs, and rarely attended any of my boy's activities. I had become agoraphobic. I had a complete fear of places and situations that might cause me the feeling of panic, helplessness or embarrassment. Staying confined to my home and not making any visits in public meant the less likely my secret life would be found out too. I penned these words knowing deep down inside that this type of living was not right but justifying it all with my diagnosis. These following words are from one of my blog writings:

> *I am sorry for all the things that we put our family members through, and I am sure most Bipolar people are, but it is what it is, and we can't dwell on the past. Don't let it destroy your relationship instead let it enhance it. Along with the bouts of anger and frustration, cycling often comes. It makes things unstable and you think there is no way a relationship can be established. Well, Noah built a boat when it had never rained before, and he did it by blind faith in God. Believing what God had promised Him and His family if only He would be faithful and do as God commanded. Low and behold, He built that boat and it began to rain. The act of believing and faith in God saved Him and His whole family.*
>
> *You and your family must have that kind of attitude. That even though I may not see the end of the road or the end to all this mess that Bipolar can be, I am going to step out by faith and believe God is with me and He will guide me and my family through. When everything is not as you dreamed it to be, and no one dreamed of being Bipolar, hopelessness can dominate your life. We can hold on with open hands, knowing that we have hope because God is faithful.*

I had become unstable and codependent with my husband. Anytime he left the house for any length of time, it was phone call after phone call or text after text bugging him with worries and concerns that were so minute. I felt the need to control everything, including him. I had to make myself believe that I was in control, but the reality was significantly different. I just kept putting on the mask day in and day out deceiving the world to who I truly was and had become, deceiving myself to the inevitable toll it was taking on my family and living in complete deception that I had things all under control. The mask was tarnishing all of my close relationships and they would plummet to the ground. I was so blinded by the masquerade and my reality was so distorted that my perception of things just being difficult for the moment was my denial of what was truly taking place behind the mask and even in the ball of my life.

# 7

## Forced Freedom

In November 2014, the annual State Meeting of Churches in Louisiana convened in Slidell, Louisiana. Jason was the moderator for the meeting, and he would always ride with or allow an older deacon to accompany him. I convinced him that I was fine and that he needed to go. Asking him to stay would only make others question what was up with me and I couldn't fathom making up an excuse or telling them the truth. So, he went, and of course, I called continuously trying to manipulate most of his time and attention. Nothing exciting or urgent was going on at home that I needed to constantly call and inform him about, but that was just the problem with my self-centered thinking. I was not receiving any attention.

All I had to do was take care of the normal household duties and our boys, and I felt the burden to not ignore my responsibilities because there was no one to take up the slack. This made me frustrated that he got to travel, and I had to stay home and clean. I got agitated that I couldn't throw a huge tantrum expressing the "unfairness" I was feeling because no one was there to see or hear it. I had no audience and there was no one to pick up the mess afterward if I made one.

I had had enough.

I called him that Friday morning and told him I couldn't take it anymore, that I could not continue living like I was. Being the concerned husband that he is and knowing my history and dark thoughts, he began to panic hearing the desperate tone in my voice. He wrapped up everything that he could at his meeting and hit the road heading toward home. He was over five hours away and I am sure his mind was filled with every bad scenario he could imagine without driving himself crazy. He called his mom to come sit with me, to make sure I was safe until he got home. I remained locked in my room, isolated from everyone. I would not dare allow an outsider to know the depth of my despair, especially my Mother in Law. It made me even more angry that he called her to come babysit me, especially since this was all his fault to start with because he left me at home.

Later that evening, Jason finally arrived home, only to find me in the bedroom, my hiding place. Lovingly, he began to talk to me but was filled with complete exhaustion and desperation. I reverted to my usual habits of verbal attacks and outlandish body gestures and had lost complete control by that point and told him I was calling the doctor once again.

That was my answer to everything- calling the doctor and getting more medicine. I had the phone in my hand about to dial the number with tears streaming down my face and fire breathing out my mouth while ice simultaneously continued forming on my heart and my reality. I had a grip on the phone like it was my lifeline to safety. I believed that there was no other help for me, but to get more medicine. I felt as if no one understood and everything would be fine as soon as I could speak to her. I was convinced that the one and only person that could truly comprehend the magnitude of my issues and sickness- my psychiatrist.

I was screaming and crying with hopelessness that I needed more medicine. I was convinced that the medications were not helping to fix me nor were they working any longer. I just had to find the right one. I had to find the right one to fix it all and make it all go away. In that one split moment, Jason's actions appeared to make all of time stop. Jason grabbed the phone out of my hands with a force and determination that he had never had with me before. He pried the phone out of my hands and said the words that I thought I would never hear. Jason said to me, "No more meds. It's me and the boys or the medicine."

The world stopped at that one exact moment or so it seemed. Did I hear him correctly? Did he really just threaten to leave me and to take my boys? What was he thinking? My family is all I have. I was livid, to say the least. The one person that was my security in life and had been silent about my little secret that I was living was now being outspoken and demanding. He was blowing the whistle on my actions. How could he? Would he? What would people think or what would he tell people about me?

It was a dark moment when I realized that the one person that had stood by my side through every tear, rage, fit, and outburst was saying no- NO MORE! In the past, he would drive me around town when the fear and anxiety were too much to bear, just trying to calm me or sometimes to find me. He was the one who held my hand thru every panic attack trying to help me breathe through them being oh, so patient with me like I was a mother in labor. He was the one I committed my life to for better or for worse. He was now saying the worst was too much to handle anymore.

What could I do? I had to get help. I had to seek out and realize through the pain of those words and anger of what felt like abandonment. There was a problem and it started with me. We got in the car and drove to the hospital once again while my mother in law stayed with the boys. It was complete and utter silence during the drive. No words were spoken, but nothing else could be said at that point.

I was just numb. I was angry, confused and completely exhausted. I had no clue how things had gotten to that point. I did not understand what was so very bad about me. I supported him in his ministry. I was a good mother to my boys and I even still kept children in my home. I was still trying to keep my masquerade on to most of the outside world and even to myself, at that moment, as I was beginning to analyze things in my head. I was trying to process everything while justifying once again, so many people live with depression and anxiety and I controlled mine in public, but I just had a little trouble in our home. I felt like a child with Attention Deficient Disorder. They are fine in school, but all that pinned up energy comes busting out at home and they go wild when they step through those doors. That seemed to be the cycle for me.

I sat in silence in the waiting room at the state hospital knowing I wouldn't be in the emergency room long because psychiatric patients go a different route than the other sick population. They called my name after sitting briefly and I felt numb, anger, confusion and just blah all at once. Most of all I was exhausted. The exhaustion of the pace of life that I had to maintain to keep my cover-up was draining.

I could maintain my composure in public, but it was a complete release and an explosion of pent up feelings in private from all the emotions. That is only when the outburst would happen. I thought to myself that it is no wonder I slept all the time, I was depleted once the gush of emotions would explode. The strength and energy it took to keep them contained and hidden from the outside world were grueling.

The nurse came in and asked the normal questions. He asked if I was suicidal or if I felt like hurting myself. This time, the answer was no to both. I just felt nothing at that point. I told him I needed to come in for a complete medicine adjustment because something was off. I could hear the patient in the room next to me talking about their suicide attempt and all of her emotional issues as if it were completely normal and thinking to myself once again about comparing to everyone else- man they are bad off.

I was still in denial at that moment and it was almost like I was living three completely different lives. The one behind the mask that experienced all the emotional issues that my husband and family would see. This Cindy included severe mood swings, anger, temper flare-ups and sleeping all the time. The second Cindy is the one on the outside of the masquerade that everyone else got to see which was always smiling and in control. She had her Bible in hand, her lipstick on, and her jewelry matching every outfit. The last Cindy is the one looking from the outside in - a self-examination. That was the one that needed to come to the forefront and dominate to be completely unbiased of the situation. I needed to examine my life as if it was not even my own. I felt like it was on a movie screen or through someone else like a Hallmark movie or on Lifetime. It felt as if I had a secret life or was a con artist not even truly understanding who those others were.

I signed the voluntary commitment paperwork knowing that would require me to stay a day or two. I then told Jason goodbye again as I entered the psychiatric ward for a second time. He was so very quiet this time and I knew he was concerned. I was wheeled by a nurse and escorted by a policeman once again up to the psychiatric floor. I thought to myself that I had been through this once before and survived so surely, I could do it again. I was positive that this would only help me to learn and acquire more tools in my toolbox for coping.

I was optimistic that maybe someone this time could find the right medicine to fix all of this.

There were two nurses working on my check-in procedures that were asking all the normal questions while checking my blood pressure, weight and going over my list of medications. The list was quite extensive. I was taking TWENTY-ONE pills a day for anxiety and depression at this point. They ranged from mood stabilizers to sleeping pills, depression medications, anxiety medicines, and benzodiazepines. I listed one by one, the milligrams and the times taken as if I was taking a roll in a classroom. It never really registered to me the abnormalcy of my medications until that split second when the psychiatric nurse looked at me and said, "And you are still functioning while taking all of this?"

My heart was screaming, "No, I am not!" and for the first time, I realized I was taking a lot of medicine and it was not normal. I didn't respond to her and I just glanced with desperation in my eyes and a blank stare. My smile was finally gone. All I could think about at that moment was whether or not my husband and boys were home packing up things to be gone when I got out.

I was then taken to a small closet sized room. It was not a typical hospital room like the last stay I had. All that was in the room was a green vinyl chair. The nurse told me that it reclined a little and that the lights would stay on and the door would be closed but there was always a camera on me. I looked around and sat there thinking that I couldn't wait until morning to get out of here. As I sat there with all my thoughts and fears and everything slowing down as the minutes ticked by, I could hear yelling from the room next to me and down the hall. It sounded like someone was in total distress, hurting, and very upset and it scared me. I had never been scared like that before and this certainly wasn't like my previous stay. <u>This was the real thing</u>. My last visit in the psychiatric ward I thought was real and that I would be well, but this time was different. This was not the nice cushy hospital room, and this was more like the psychiatric ward that you see on the movies for those truly mentally unstable. I was a patient there, and I was there for a reason.

They wouldn't allow me to have anything with me like last time so all I had was my thoughts and prayers. The one and only thing I could do to hold back all my fears was to pray. All I could do was to cry out from the deepest, darkest, and loneliest pit of my heart with my desperate, restless, and for once, finally completely honest prayers. For those few hours that seemed like an eternity, I cried and cried out to Jesus asking for help. Pouring out every hidden secret, fear, and worry that I believed to be concealed from everyone. God gave me the courage and strength to take off my masquerade for the first time in many many years MAYBE EVER. I believed that I was hiding from everyone about my problem, but truly was only hiding from myself.

I got real that night. I got real with my Savior and Creator, and I got real with myself. As I cried and prayed, I felt as if layer by layer my mask was being peeled back from the weight and burden of wearing the masquerade. After wearing it for so many years, it was now beginning to shed off. The masquerade began to fade that night in that tiny fluorescent-lit suicide watch room in the psychiatric ward on November 14, 2014.

After a few hours, the nurse came and got me and said that it was time to meet with the doctors. I thought to myself, "Doctors, now we are getting somewhere." So, she took me to another small room where I walked in with six different doctors. There were men and women all in white jackets sitting around the room. Each one had my file in one hand and a pen in the other. It was very intimidating as if I was going to be read my last rights. They asked me to be seated and I sat right in the middle with some on my right side and a few on my left. Two were positioned straight in front of me.

I remember the very first question from the main doctor. He had dark skin and studious glasses on his face, his bleached white lab coat and a cheap Bic pen in hand. His first question to me was, "Why are you here?" Well, that was a loaded question to me, and I really was only here because I needed to keep my husband and family. I needed help keeping my family together and to find out what is wrong with me desiring to know why I couldn't cope with life. But that was not my answer I gave him, the answer that rolled off my tongue with fire and force and with the purest of convictions stated, "I want off all of the meds."

The look on the doctor's face was non-emotional. He didn't say to me what every previous doctor had said, and he didn't say that it was impossible. He didn't try to convince me that I needed them, and he didn't say the famous go to line when people talk about depression medications that they were needed like a cast for my broken brain or necessary like a pill for my high blood pressure. He didn't try to persuade me that they were crucial to stabilize the chemicals in my brain that were not functioning and firing as they should. He simply said, 'Ok!"

He and the others began asking me about my previous "bipolar" diagnosis and what actions or behaviors that attributed to the doctor coming to that conclusion. He interrogated me about what I did when I would swing from a depression state to a manic episode. I went back over all the details of being sad, upset, and lonely to just being very creative and artistic. Several other questions came from around the room and I answered each with to the best of my ability with confusion as to why they were asking so many questions about the bipolar. I was being completely honest and raw for the first time. I felt like I was taking a test. I hoped that I would pass.

They then went over my medications one by one and asked why I was on it. It was an extensive list and to go over all of them took some time. There were several times that I would just have to answer honestly with, "I don't know why I am taking this. I guess just the depression and anxiety." I was shocked as they explained how some of the medications were used for pain and neuropathy. I was puzzled as to why I was taking those. Things began to register with me as each prescription was discussed. I completed all of the questions that they had at that time and the lead doctor told me that they would see me in a little bit after they came up with a game plan.

I was hopeful for the first time in many many years because someone was actually asking me what I wanted and why. They were looking at me and my medical history with fresh eyes and scanning through my extensive list of medications. These doctors allowed me to have a voice and hope. The hope to not just be a medical diagnosis or a number on a chart, but to actually have hope to not accept that this is the way that life had to be for me.

As I left the room, feeling utter exhaustion from being emotionally drained and the lack of sleep, I decided it was time to call Jason. I went into the hallway where the public phone was and dialed his number.

My heart was fluttering, and I knew his voice would calm every fear and nerve. I believed his words of encouragement and love would put me at peace like they had so many times before. He answered the phone and I was relieved. I had been terrified that he wouldn't even answer, and I tried being my bubbly self and apologized profusely for putting him through this again. I was receiving only one-word answers from him and a tone of what appeared, to me, to be anger. I told him the doctors were very nice and that they were going to find just the right combination of meds to make things all better. I don't recall the rest of the conversation, but what I thought I heard him say to me again was, "Not all the meds." I began panicking on the phone because of my perception of what my husband was saying was that he was never going to allow me to come home while I was on medication.

I began crying and begging him to forgive me and he just kept answering me with such short, non-emotional answers and insisting that I needed help. As I hung up the phone, I was in a complete panic at this point and I slowly walked back down to my room dragging my feet. I knew I had told the doctors I wanted off medicine, but I didn't really mean "all" of them. I knew there was absolutely no way that I could function without medication after being on some of them for thirteen years.

A social worker came into my room and talked to me about some counseling and action plans for when I left the hospital and I had no clear answers to give her. I wasn't even sure if I had a family or home to return to. In the middle of our meeting, the nurse came into my room and said the doctors wanted to meet with me again. I was puzzled but hopeful at that moment and my thoughts raced as I walked back down the hall. Could they have found the magic pill or a cure for me?

I sat down in the same chair with the future of my life waiting to be dictated to me by these doctors. The decision that they had made was about to be revealed to me. It was the verdict that was going to secure my home and family or terminate it. The lead doctor began talking to me about how bipolar disorder is frequently misdiagnosed. He said that a "label" or "medical code" must be placed on patients for doctors to know which route to take for treatment or to justify to insurance companies and medical boards why they are doing what they are doing.

Then, the badge of shame-yet justification of actions label, that I wore for so many years was the topic discussed. He clearly stated, "You are NOT bipolar. We are clearly taking that diagnosis away." I sat there in disbelief. In utter shock, that for 13 years I had lived a lie and made that mental disease diagnosis become a self-fulfilling prophecy by my actions. He said, "I do believe you have circumstantial depression and may have needed some of these medications for a certain time period, but none of them were ever intended for long term use and especially not for the time frame or years that I had been taking most of them."

The chains of bondage that I had been tethered to were slowly starting to loosen at that very moment and I was in disbelief to what I was hearing. Was this really coming true? He said that they had created an action plan for me to get off everything, if I was up for it, and if I was really serious about wanting to get off all of the medications. I said of course as if I was just offered the keys to a second chance at my life and my marriage.

He had it all written down in very detailed steps and told me the seriousness and health precautions that I needed to take because of the risks that were involved stopping some of them. He said it would be very difficult getting off some of the medicines with my body being so dependent and suggested that I be monitored 24 hours a day for a few days because of the risk of seizures and the withdrawal symptoms that I would experience.

All of that information was whirling in my head because all I could think was "Is this real? Am I really going to be free?" I had prayed so many times to be healed from bipolar disorder and now it was being answered by the removal of the diagnosis. I knew I did not need to be home during this withdrawal process and needed to be away from the environment that may trigger negative emotions. I also needed to spare my husband and boys from seeing or experiencing any more trauma that could happen as a result of the detoxing.

They told me to work on an action plan for going home and we would go from there. I left in shock with butterflies of excitement. I went into the dayroom to call Jason again and there were three other patients in there when I entered. One female was giving the other two a lesson on how to beat the system and get more medications. I dialed his number in nervous excitement and he answered again. I told him that I was going to do this. I was going to get off the medications. Something was going to be different this time and I had hope, determination, and I wasn't making excuses anymore.

I acknowledged that I couldn't ask to come home nor did I want to. I mentioned going to my sister's house in Arkansas. She has a loving and nurturing nature but could keep me structured and on the right track. He said he would talk to her and see if that was a possibility. For once, after this struggle and battle for so many years, it felt as if there were hope and light at the end of my tunnel.

A few meetings and discussions occurred between doctors and social workers. Things were in place for my release, and a plan was devised to allow me to stop taking medications. I had not been given any that morning, so the anxiousness and jittery feelings were building. I realized it would immediately require "self-talking" to avoid a breakdown before even being dismissed from the hospital. A breakdown would halt my going home!

The doctors took me off nineteen pills that day. It was seven different medications that I stopped taking immediately, and many of them I took different doses throughout the day. I was given anti-nausea medication, if needed, to help with the possible withdrawal, detox symptoms. Now I had a plan to wean off the last two pills over the course of the next three days along with stopping the newly added medication. I was terrified, anxious and definitely starting, what I now know to be, some withdrawal symptoms. I was informed that I would have them and many would not be pleasant. My body had become dependent on these medications, for many years, and now I was saying NO MORE. So, of course, my body was going to go into shock and distress.

I went to the nurse's station to receive my discharge orders and they had to take my vitals one last time before I left. I took a deep breath knowing my pulse was faster than normal experiencing every emotion known to man at that moment. I was filled with so many different emotions: excited to be free, scared to fail, anxious facing the world medicine free, nervous engaging with my husband, and vulnerable to be raw and label-free. I was also very embarrassed that I had lived out a diagnosis that wasn't even true. Hiding behind medications or a mental disease diagnosis was no longer an option. I now had to take personal responsibility for my actions and reactions.

My pulse was elevated, my blood pressure was high, and my breathing had started to become more labored. The nurse was so gracious and patient with me and knew I was nervous. She did not record the first one and said that she would redo it in just a few moments. She told me to imagine my happy place to slow my breathing down, and she would take it again. I did just that. I closed my eyes and thoughts of my husband, my boys, my mom, and all the people that God had blessed me with flooded my mind.

Then I started imagining the clouds and the gentle breeze moving them slowly across the sky. I have always loved the outdoors and I remember for hours as a kid laying in the grass staring at the clouds and making animals and things out of them. Even as I am typing this, I am sitting in my sunroom with the door wide open listening to the bird's chirp, the wind blowing the leaves on the trees and the gentle breeze in the air. I imagined everything in the world being as it should be-calm and at peace.

The nurse took it for a second time just a few minutes later, but it seemed like forever to me because my thoughts had changed so drastically in a short amount of time. My heart rate had slowed and my tight shoulders that were drawn up from stress had slowly dropped and were now relaxed. I was calm and at peace. I felt a bit of pride as she recorded the numbers. They had returned back to normal. It was my first step in learning to be in control of myself. I did it! I was personally responsible for myself and my emotions.

She told me everything was good, and I could go home. I was ready to bust out of that place and leave the psychiatric ward behind with all of the myriad emotions that I had experienced in the last twenty-four hours. My deepest, darkest and scariest pit of my entire life was that night I spent in that hospital. On the other side of that, it was the place where I literally felt the peace of God come over me and give me hope like never before. Joy truly did come in the morning!

November 15, 2014, will forever be a special day in my heart and in our family's lives. It is so special that we celebrate it every year. That is the date I wear on a ring on my left-hand pointer finger. It is my D-Day.

My deliverance day! The day that the bondage of hiding behind the masquerade, the diagnosis and labels and the addiction to medications were delivered and I was set free. I was now going to dance at my ball with no mask with a totally different beat of music than I had ever even heard.

Jason and I walked out of the hospital as I was still very drained and slightly overwhelmed with all the many different emotions. As soon as we start walking outside of the hospital to head to the car, we ran into some lifelong friends of ours. I looked horrible after sleeping in a chair all night long, crying for hours and certainly no makeup. I had not brushed my teeth, my clothes were wrinkled and worn, and I didn't even have my hair brushed. There was no running, no hiding, and no disguising this time. This was my first true test. My first encounter was raw and there was nowhere to run and hide.

They were there because their mother had been admitted and Jason came to my defense and covered for me quickly when asked what we were up to. He just answered stating that I had been sick. Technically, that wasn't a lie. I was sick just not the way that they probably thought.

You see, I was addicted to prescription medications. I never abused the medicine in the essence of taking more than I was prescribed, but I did misuse them as a coping mechanism. You don't get to a point of taking 21 pills without having an addiction problem. I used the medicine to try and fix my heart, numb it or just to paralyze all my emotions. I was addicted to the ritualistic routine of taking medication. I did experience true depression at different times of my life and I never gave myself the ability to grieve my mother's passing. I suppressed too many emotions and feelings.

I hid them all behind my mask never truly dealing with anything. I compare all the hiding behind the smile and the masquerade like sweeping dirt under the rug in the living room. It's fine for a day or two but eventually, as you keep doing that and adding bigger clumps of trash, rocks, and dirt, the rug starts to get bulky and things start to seep out. Eventually, all the dust will just start busting from underneath the seams because it can't hide it all anymore and the rug has now become a tripping hazard for those walking by.

That had become my life. What was once true, legitimate, horrible events in my life, that never got dealt with, had now become huge boulders of trash and dirt that I was trying to maintain under my control and hidden. Honestly, all of my doctors through the years were only going by my own descriptions and information about my emotions and how I was feeling. They were told what I was choosing to tell them because there is no blood test or perfect exam to diagnosis mental disorders. No blame or fault to any them. I would strictly give them the worst symptoms or what I would choose to disclose and many times downplaying the severity of my condition of what occurred behind closed doors. I would never dig deep enough getting down to the root cause of everything because that required personal responsibility.

Masquerade wearing had become my life. The neatly placed smile that I would even put on at the doctor's office was so harmful to my healing through the years. Being me was all I had to do, but I didn't know how to stop being who everyone expected. I was a habitual mask wearer that could have cost me my husband, my boys and my life. Taking it off was one of the scariest things to ever do but freeing at the same time. God created me to shine and not to hide my light under a bushel and certainly not behind a masquerade.

# 8

## Mask Drop

Here we go back to the timeline, I went to my sister's house taking only three pills. Much like an ex-smoker that has decided to quit, they continue to fiddle with their fingers or repeat the behaviors or ticks associated with smoking, I too lived in habitual behaviors surrounding my medicine taking. I lived by the clock and when I should take what pills. It was hard not to look at the clock every five minutes to see when I needed to take my next anxiety medicine because there weren't any to take anymore.

I had to break all my old habits. I had to train myself much like I would train a puppy or a small child. Action and reaction to most situations are learned behaviors. When something works or gets the response that we want then we continue doing it and if not then we stop. I had to train myself to learn how to cope with life in constructive ways without the medications. I got the reaction and feedback I desired, which was attention, when I acted inappropriately because I had a diagnosis to blame everything on. Now I no longer had that as a crutch to fall back on.

I now had to face reality and everything that came along with that, because I was finally allowing myself to be honest and not trying to justify my actions or please everyone else. Hearing myself verbalize my true weaknesses was liberating. I acknowledged that I had control issues and I realized that I acted out impulsively to get the response from others that I wanted. Blaming everything on the diagnosis and the medicine had been my predetermined excuse instead of taking any personal responsibility.

After leaving the hospital, I went to my sister's house to recover. During my stay with my sister, my sweet niece gave up her room for me to sleep in and to have my own private space with a bathroom while I was there. It was a colorful, girly room that was cheerful and happy. I loved it because it was a nice change for me since I only had boys. As I entered the room and started unpacking my bag, I was disillusioned that I was just there for a friendly family visit. I didn't realize the magnitude of what I was going to experience over the next few days. It had been explained to me by the doctors, but words being explained on a medical level and the actual experience are two completely different things.

My sister made index cards with encouraging scriptures and placed them all around the room. One was placed on the little nightstand next to the bed exactly eye level when laying in the bed. Several were on the bathroom mirror and one was even on the refrigerator. Without me even realizing it, she was covering me in God's word and my mind was being filled with truth as I glanced at those words over and over for the next several days.

I have always had trouble sleeping and was no longer taking the prescription medication for insomnia. I knew learning to sleep without medicines would be a struggle. On the first evening, I situated all my things and decided to go to bed. It had been a long emotionally challenging several days, years to be exact, and I just wanted to rest. I got settled in bed and my sister came in to talk. She had bought me a book and had written the sweetest message inside of how she knew I was going to be a conqueror through this, and she prayed for me that night. She covered me with love through her prayer and sent me to off to sleep with a focused, peaceful but tired mind frame.

I don't remember if I called Jason before I went to bed that night, but I had already settled in my mind that I was not going to bug him every five minutes like I had made it a habit of doing. This was a journey that I had to take on my own and I needed to learn how to do it. I tossed and turned all night long. I began the withdrawal symptoms pretty much at the hospital, but I was not prepared for what I was going to experience over the next few days.

I began tossing and turning in bed as sweat began to pour out of my system. At first, that was easy to explain away because I was just hot natured. Everyone keeps the temperature of their house at different levels, but not quite that different. Sweat was pouring out of my body like I was sitting in a sauna. I was tearing off the sheets and blankets to try and cool my body down. The cool air that filled the room would shock my system. As the cool air hit me, then I switched from pouring sweat to shivering then the shivering went back to sweats repeatedly.

I then decided to go and shower trying to relax and to somehow regulate my body temperature. I put the water on the hottest that I could possibly set it. As I am standing there letting the water wash over me, my mind is racing between the thoughts of being able to survive all of this and if I really had the strength to endure. The self-doubt started weighing heavily on me. As I am washing up, my stomach begins to churn, and I am thinking maybe my supper just didn't settle well with me. I quickly finished up because I knew I was going to be sick and I was. I have always had a nervous stomach, but this was detox sick...totally different and much worse. I finished up in the bathroom and decided to try and settle back down in bed.

The wave of exhaustion hit again, and I knew I needed to rest. I snuggled back in bed and glanced over at the nightstand where the little scripture index card was placed. I could barely read it with the small lamp light that was on. The scripture that was there was Psalm 73:26, "My flesh and my heart faileth: but God is the strength of my heart, and my portion forever." Little did I know that would be the verse that I would cling to over the next several days. My flesh was failing, and my heart was weary and worn ridden with doubt and fear, but I knew I could not fail. If I failed, I knew I was I going to lose my family. But then those two little words positioned right in the middle were the key to that verse "But God." The first part of the verse is bleak and hopeless, but that conjunction statement doesn't let the story end on a bad note. The remaining part of the verse is what I needed to learn and to live. "That God is the strength of my heart and my portion forever."

So during the night as my head began to pound, my eyes were burning from the continuous crying that occurred over the last several days, my legs began to kick and cramp and my body temperature fluctuated drastically, I just kept saying over and over as I drifted off to sleep sometime during the night, "My flesh and my heart may fail. But God is my strength."

I woke up the next morning and my sister had breakfast made and was sitting at the kitchen table. My appetite was poor from all the things that my body was going through, but I mustered up the ability to eat a little.

Over the next several days, I experienced several different withdrawal symptoms as my body weaned off the dependence of all the medications. I have experienced some long-term memory blockage from all the medication for so many years. It's as if part of my life had been erased. That long term side effect paled in comparison to the immediate withdrawal symptoms that I experienced after leaving the hospital. I had a frequent feeling of bugs crawling on me, but nothing would be there. The brain fog and lack of concentration came and went and many times I felt as if I was moving in slow motion through the thickest mire and mud possible.

The sweats would hit with my face being flush and on fire and water seeping out of my pores so much that my hair would be soaked. Then, the opposite, freezing and having goosebumps come up on all over my body and staying for a while to the point of hurting. They were so intense that the little bumps would make me sensitive to touch and my skin would turn a purplish color. I also had some major stomach issues over the next few days going from intense cramps, vomiting, and diarrhea. My body was definitely going through a major shock and it was reminding me of the poison that had been in my system for many years.

On that first full day after being out of the hospital, my sister made me put on my tennis shoes and go walking with her. I really wanted to just stay in bed, but I felt I needed to oblige her and at least try. Plus, I knew she wouldn't take no for an answer. We walked every day for the next several days and she kept encouraging me to increase my pace. As I increased my pace, my heart rate started to increase and that was not a comfortable response for me.

That feeling was scary to me because it mimicked the feeling that I had in the middle of a panic attack. But again, she didn't take no for an answer and told me that it was a good feeling because it meant my heart was working and assured me that I was not going to die. As my pace got faster, my breathing rhythm became more labored. This was still very unsettling for me, but she kept reminding me that I was fine. She was constantly assuring me that as long as I was breathing, and my heart was beating it meant that my heart was working, and my lungs were doing the job they were created to do.

I hated to hear that answer each day as she made me walk outside around the church parking lot or in the church gym if weather conditions were not favorable. She kept saying the sweat pouring from my system was good and healthy and that it was my fat crying and getting rid of all those toxins. I tried believing what she had to say, but all I was doing at that moment was trying to keep her off my case.

I would wake up early, make myself shower, and tried getting myself in some sort of routine. The withdrawal symptoms would vary between an upset stomach, diarrhea, sweating, and severe trouble concentrating. It felt at times like I was in a bubble in an alternate reality as people were talking all around me. I would watch and observe them from the inside but not quite sure how to act or respond. I wasn't confident in my actions or responses or that I was even processing everything correctly. I would call Jason from time to time and we would discuss things about the boys and how they were doing. I would question what they were thinking and always concerned not to be too emotional while talking with him. I didn't want to appear like I didn't have it under control or that there had not been any changes made.

When Sunday rolled around, I decided to go to church, but I knew I was not ready for Sunday School. I was concerned about facing the crowd and especially people that I was not really familiar with, but knew I needed to go. I went and a few inquired as to why I was in and I just answered that I needed to come visit my sister. I cried a lot during that service reflecting on how I had let things get so bad and decline to this horrific level. I was struggling with my selfish thoughts that surrounded me, my hurts, my needs, and my battles.

I weaned off my last medications over the first three days at my sister's house and was now completely drug-free. I had not been this way in over thirteen years. Knowing it would take a while for my body to adjust and function normally, I never realized going cold turkey off nineteen pills was going to be so hard. It was everything you see on television on intervention shows and more.

Withdrawals are just that- your body going into shock and rebelling against you. You have denied it by not giving it the one thing it is used to and is craving. I experienced, felt and thought everything you could imagine while going through my withdrawal week. But I survived. I stayed on the course only by the grace of God and survived only by reciting over and over in my heart, my head, and out of my lips, "My flesh and my heart may fail, but God is my strength and my portion forever."

Jason and I both agreed that it was time for me to come home after staying with my sister for a week. It was a mutual decision that is was not in the best interest of, appropriate for, and too scary for the kids to see everything that I went through. So, staying with my sister was the best choice. Most of the withdrawal symptoms had ceased at this point and I am now very thankful that Jason did not see me in that state and that I proved to myself that I had the strength through Christ to succeed. My sister had taken off work for a few days so she could closely monitor me and after those few days, I was beginning to become clear headed and able to focus and think. At this point, I was out of any life-threatening danger that could have occurred and was now ready to return home.

Jason came and picked me up from my sister's and the ride home was awkward, to say the least. The fear of saying the wrong things and holding a grudge were legitimate concerns. I did not want the sting of the ultimatum that was given to me by my husband to be brewing down deep in my heart. I tried to suppress all negative emotions and wished to demonstrate love by being cordial, upbeat and honest. I honestly was giving it every effort but there was definitely some distance between us. The wall between us was noticeable and only time would tell to prove to him that I was committed to make this life change and to earn my husband's trust back.

We stopped to eat lunch and then traveled on until we made it back to our home. He informed me during the drive that he had flushed all my medications down the toilet. I was shocked for a split second, but then very thankful that he took that initiative. Thankful that he went ahead and did that so I wouldn't have to face all the brown bottles laying all over the counters. As I was unpacking my things, I did find an older bottle with a few pills still remaining and I flushed them myself.

The days and weeks to come were not easy because I was having to learn how to discover who I was and to learn my place and position in the home and in our marriage. I was determined to discover who I truly was finally being unmedicated. The anxiety would build up from just everyday pressures and I would go lay in bed and pray and listen to Kari Jobe's song, "You Are Not Alone." That became my go-to song as I felt myself getting overwhelmed and not able to handle the pressure. That was now my new constructive habit to run to instead of taking a pill, throwing a fit, or having an anxiety attack.

I did slip up a time or two with getting overwhelmed and taking my stress out on others. The panic attacks lessened and when they would come Jason would talk me through them just like that nurse had taught me using the five senses tactic. They occurred less and less as I became more aware of myself, my actions, my triggers, and that I could control my reactions.

Wearing the masquerade was easier for me than allowing myself to be accountable for my actions. The mask was stripped off and the diagnosis erased so the real me had to be rediscovered. It wasn't easy because my ball which I refer to as my life was still the same. The same home, the same family, the same church and the same friends, but the one factor that wasn't the same was me. I was maskless!

# Mask in Hand

Learning to live maskless was just that a learning process. This new life was like a blister that has rubbed on the back of your heel from your brand-new shoes. You couldn't wait to have them, so you put them on immediately after purchasing because you are that excited, and of course, they perfectly compliment your outfit. Never considering that you need to break them in before walking around Disney World or shopping all day. The blister is a nice big bubble and you go to your handy dandy pharmacy store buying those new bandages to protect and cushion it. No matter how hard you try for it not to, the blister pops, and the fresh skin underneath is just very raw and sensitive. It takes time to heal while the new skin grows and forms sometimes leaving a calloused area and other times absolutely no evidence that it was even there. But the process to healing was painful nonetheless, as my journey has been.

The journey to wellness is never over and as I have walked this road over the last few years, I have learned that God did create emotions. Ecclesiastes 3:4-6 clearly tells us, "A time to weep, and a time to laugh; a time to mourn, and a time to dance; a time to cast away stones, and a time to gather stones together; a time to embrace, and a time to refrain from embracing; A time to get, and a time to lose; a time to keep, and a time to cast away; A time to rend, and a time to sew; a time to keep silence, and a time to speak; A time to love, and a time to hate; a time of war, and a time of peace."

My mask had been forced off and my true self was exposed to others.

Instead of being ashamed that I had struggles and different emotions with the seasons of my life, I needed to learn that there is a time for everything. I should have wept properly when my Mother passed on instead of suppressing my feelings because I knew she was in Heaven. I needed to learn to laugh at life and even my mistakes because I was not perfect, and none were fatal. I had mourned losing my mother, but I depended on her for all of my emotional support and I needed to learn to dance on my own. I cast stones at certain personal relationships with those close to me pushing them away and not allowing people to get to know the true me and my true heart. Now it was time to gather those relationships back together. I needed to learn to embrace those things that were productive in my life and refrain from bad behaviors. I needed to learn to get in touch with myself and who God would want me to be and to lose the doubts and insecurities of who Satan had convinced me I was.

I chose to keep my family and cast away the dependence on medications. It was time to rend the wasted time. It was time to sow a beautiful life with new memories together. It was time to keep my excuses silent and instead speak about the deliverance God had brought me through. It was time for me to love- love my God, myself and my family. It was now time for me to hate what I had allowed my life to become and the way that I allowed Satan to rob from me for so many years. It was a time of war on Satan and his lies and a time for me to know how to truly have peace. "Peace that passes all understanding" because my masquerade was off, and I was now attending a new ball in my life. I was repeating verses over and over in my head knowing that my flesh and my heart may truly and literally fail- BUT God is my strength and my portion forever.

No one, including myself, is broken beyond repair or beyond the reach of God's love and amazing grace. People are not inherently evil because they have an addiction, hidden secrets, or sins that they struggle with. Many people have a mental disorder or a diagnosis that has given them no hope for normalcy by the medical community. Others may battle depression or anxiety only with different seasons in their lives or maybe every stinking day just like I did. No matter what you are dealing with, what you have been told by someone with all the degrees hanging on their walls, or the bad hand that you have been dealt in this life, you must tell them all "But God!" I had too and so can you!

I did not walk around with a needle in my arm like the addicts that you see on television. I did not walk down back alleys to make deals to get more medicine than was prescribed to feed my need. However, even if you are one of those people that must do those things, there is healing, forgiveness, and grace for you just like there was for me. I did good things for others and was a great person at times that loved the Lord even with all my trials and my secrets.

I knew all the right answers, but I quit relying on and applying those answers. I didn't realize the answer in Luke 9:23, "And he said to them all, If any man will come after me, let him deny himself, and take up his cross daily, and follow me." I missed out on the five-letter word "daily" and only did it on the really bad days.

Part of the healing process was reflecting and realizing where I was, to begin with. I went back and searched all my old posts and journal entries and as I am sharing with you in this chapter my intentions to wellness were pure and honest. I never intentionally set out to go down the road that I did, nor did I mean for the journey to take so long to return back to safety, but I am sure glad that I did.

This short journal entry shows my heart was willing, but I didn't realize just how weak my emotions were.

> *I learned that I needed to change my vocabulary and not use "I can't!" anymore. Why do you say I can't? Because we use that as an excuse to not do things that are a little hard or uncomfortable. We use our disease as a crutch.*

Some of my writings from the past are painful to me and sadden me that I was heading in the right direction each and every time, but I just couldn't maintain the momentum, fight the addiction, or keep my eyes focused on Jesus for any length of time. I didn't keep up the good healing habits to fight the daily battles. Why is it that the things we know to do that will help us in the long run, we don't do? Yet we do things that we know are not healthy and not good for us. The long-term success is the testimony of our daily habits and that's where I struggled. The Bible tells us "A double minded man is unstable in all his ways." (James 1:8) and "Therefore to him, that knoweth to do good, and doeth *it* not, to him it is sin." (James 4:17) We all agree with these verses until we must personally apply them to ourselves. I am so thankful that today I still believe these words that I typed back in 2011 on my blog.

> *I leave you with these words of a song by Shelia Walsh, "Are you weary, are you frightened? When you go to bed, do you leave the light on? When the cold wind blows to disturb your peace, do you lock the door so no else can see? Broken promises have left their mark on you. In your unbelief, one thing you must hold on to.*
>
> *When the road becomes too rough, when you're ready to give up, when you're crying out for love, God is faithful. When your peace cannot be found, He will never let you down, you have chosen solid ground. God is faithful."*

I am forever thankful and richly blessed that my husband and family never gave up on me. I put all of them through some very difficult times throughout the years. As you have been reading, more than most of you ever realized. I am still amazed and forever grateful that they stood beside me for the long haul. The most important fact of all is that Jesus never left me, and he knew the real me behind the mask and still loved me. I thought the masquerade was protection for myself and keeping everyone at a distance from my heart, but I did not realize the wreckage that I was causing in my relationships with others and losing myself in the process. These following words were written in my journal as my cry for help, but I just didn't know how to actually ask for it.

> *I would use the words, "I can't," way too much as an excuse for not going. It is too hard to go and put the mask on of happiness when deep down inside I was crumbling.*

I should have been mature enough to see all the warning signs. When I would write in my journal and call out for help in one line and then I would praise Jesus in the next. This is a prime example of the two-sided person that I had become:

> *I have had a rough few days with low self-esteem and depression and my anxiety has heightened. I didn't know what to do. I was worrying that I was spiraling downwards, and I didn't want that to happen. I didn't want to fall into the deep pit again. I didn't really know why I was feeling this way, there was no rhyme or reason. Nothing had happened to make me feel this way.*
>
> *I felt like a hypocrite because I had been so good, and I had been praising His name. Now here I was not adhering to my own advice. I did the only thing I knew to do was ask people to pray for me. I ask friends to pray for my mood and my state of mind. I have a great support system of people that love the Lord, and I believe they did because I slept all night last night and I woke up refreshed and ready to face the world today. No more depression.*
>
> *When low self-esteem and doubt paralyze us, we can give up and accept the distorted image, or we can remember who we are in Christ. We are loved most of all. When we are in a depressive state or feeling low (because some won't admit it is depression), we have a Heavenly Father who cares. He cares and he uses people in our lives to show us sometimes when we can't see them ourselves.*

Praise God that He gave courage to my family and friends to keep faith and hope. I am thankful that God wasn't finished with me yet. I am still perplexed by the thought that I was screaming for help on the inside but was unable to honestly verbalize the truth to someone on the outside. I felt like that 5th-grade little girl all over again that had received her first F. I didn't want to disappoint anyone or to be considered a failure. I didn't understand why I couldn't take off the masquerade and let everyone see my normal human fears, frailties, and imperfections. Most of the time I was too afraid, too comfortable, too justified by a diagnosis, and too self-reliant to stop wearing the mask. As the following journal entry proves, I was straddling the fence between real-world reality and my own created reality.

> *I read a statement the other day that really caught my attention. You must take your garbage out when it gets full. The garbage man does not come in and get it for you. Neither will God! But if we confess it, He has promised to pick it up and throw it away. If you keep it in, your house gets stinky.*
>
> *So, it is the same way with the things that we put in our minds. The kind of music we listen to, the tv shows and movies we watch. What we fill our minds with will come out. Romans 12:2 states, "And be not conformed to this world, but be ye transformed by the renewing of your mind, that ye may prove what is that good, and acceptable, and perfect, will of God." Now, this is not an instant process. This is a daily transformation of ourselves to be more and more like Jesus.*
>
> *With depression the mind can get boggled up with negativity and confusion, but "If we live in the Spirit. let us also walk in the Spirit." (Galatians 5:25) Satan likes to put snares out there for us and get our focus inwardly and not outwardly on Christ.*
>
> *From experience, I lived way too many years listening to the voice of the Devil and all his lies. His voice overshadowed anything and everything I knew as a Christian. I believed his lies and therefore he had me in bondage of depression. My Deliverer set me free by breaking me and molding me into a vessel that can be used for Him.*
>
> *Now I am not saying that I am perfect by any means nor is God through making and molding me, but I am daily learning how to walk in the Spirit. Now I know that all my problems are not always from being bipolar, but some are from being away from the will of God. I still struggle with the issues of being bipolar and the anxiety issues, but if I will remember I have a Father who cares and wants to help me through the storms.*

As you can see, I recognized the spiritual aspect of my healing even back in October of 2011, before the diagnosis was taken away, but it's easier to preach a sermon to others than to adhere to it ourselves.

> *A mask can be a tricky thing. It can be used for both good and bad. It disguises us into something else. I decided a long time ago to stop wearing a mask. Now there are certain situations where I have to put one on for another person's good or well-being, but for the most part, I don't.*
>
> *When we take our masks off, we can recognize each other's pain. We become transparent and sometimes vulnerable, but if it is to help someone else, then why not. Isn't that what we are called to do?*
>
> *I don't go around with a sign that says, "I am Bipolar." I do however share with those who ask or are going through a tough time. I share how far I have come by the grace of God. I can share my experiences. We go through things to learn from them and grow, and if I can make someone else's journey a little easier I will.*

May of 2012, I continued wearing that mask just piling on the layers of denial, self-depreciation, and justification of my actions. Rehearsing all the right words to say in my head, but not wanting to truly personally apply them as if I was an actress repeating a script. This blog writing proves that,

> *I got back in touch with an old friend today and it brought back many memories. All very good ones, I might add, but it got me to thinking about what if's? I live sometimes on what if's? What if I didn't have to live on pills because of the Bipolar? What would life be like? Been there done that not going back. What if I could work a full-time job again and not struggle with money? God has me at this place in my life for a reason. So, I could go on and on with the what ifs. Many are very big decisions in my life, and some are very small, but I can't live on the what if's. I must accept each*

and every day as a gift from God and live it to the best of my ability for Him. Who knows what He has in store for me in the future, but in His word, it tells us to be content. So, I accept my place in life at this time and strive to do His will each and every day that He gives me. So not what if -what will? What will I do with this time for Him?

Many times, days and for years, I would pray for healing from the awful disease and diagnosis, but never imagined that there would be a day where I would or could be medicine free. I didn't understand the magnitude of God and the fact that He is living inside of me. That the One that spoke the world into existence was the same One that wanted me to cry out to Him for help. He was waiting with open arms. I just needed to jump into them. I knew how to say it, teach others about it, but wasn't quite sure how to do it myself.

> In the battle of life, we must CHOOSE. Choose to take medication because we know it is better for us than the alternative. Choose to go to counseling because we know it will help ourselves and our family. Choose to exercise because we know it will help the depression and all over mindset, but I did not say the choice would be easy or likable. I don't often like these things, but I know they are best for me. We must Choose to do what's right even when everyone else is doing wrong or telling us otherwise.
>
> I read a quote this week that just pierced my heart. Control the controllable and let God control the uncontrollable. That is such a profound statement. There are many things in my life that I can control; however, there are circumstances and things that are just not in my territory they are God's. I need to let Him control them. Now being a little OCD about things that is very hard, but that is the only way to find true peace and harmony in my life.
>
> I need to say "Whatever!" Lord, more often. Not in the demeaning way but giving up my life to Him. Whatever in the sense that I am His, and He is ultimately and

*completely in control. So, on those down days when I can't seem to get it all together, I can roll with the punches as my mood swings and realize that I can't control everything. God does!*

But you see, there were things that I could control, and I just didn't want to. I personally chose not to. It was easier to be blinded and look the other way than to do the hard work. Now, I do believe the Biblical truth that "I can do ALL things through Christ which strengtheneth me." (Philippians 4:13) I believe it and I now live it despite what label is placed on me or what medical statistics say that I should be doing or would never be able to do. Through that strength in Christ, I defied the odds and the labels and am still medicine free.

Many of my journal entries were God's word trying to speak to me and penetrate my own heart. It was as if my heart and the true Cindy had become like winter. Cold, dreary and everything appearing to be dead and gone, but underneath deep down inside beneath the layer of winter are the flowers, trees and beautiful evidence of Spring holding on to burst through in God's timing. God was there, and the truth of his word was under the layers upon layers of the masquerade, but I just wouldn't allow it to burst through as I just kept asserting my "words of wisdom" onto everyone else to follow.

*I think we are often the same in our Christian life. We get so used to seeing things our way that when God speaks to us, we don't even recognize His voice. We squint through life, like I did, and we often forget the big picture of what we were created for. We get so bogged down with our own issues, problems, and opinions that God's plan can't be seen.*

*We need to have a spiritual eye exam and see if we are seeing Him clearly. We need to look at things through God's eyes not our own. Our own is often ruled by the flesh and we need to be ruled by the Spirit. Sometimes we just need to stop and recognize who God is and who we truly are in Him. Our vision is not clear unless we look through God's eyes, not our own, and not just to see His will but also do it.*

"While we look not at the things which are seen, but at the things which are not seen: for the things which are seen are temporal; but the things which are not seen are eternal." (2 Corinthians 4:18) I could not see how my story was going to end or where I would be. I had to allow God to give me an eye examination as my eyes were opened, washed out and fixed on the eternal.

This writing was from 2015 about a year after stopping all the medications.

> *I can remember vividly the day I realized there was really BAD people in this world. Our family had just come home from a week at Church Camp with a week of encouragement and spiritual refreshment and we had to have a family meeting. When the family gathered in my parents' bed, you knew something was up. Someone had been stealing money out of our bank account. My parents worked tirelessly to try and prove it wasn't us and someone else had done it. Come to find out it was someone from another state. These were the days before fraud services, but our family survived. It was a terrible situation that had happened to our family for a hard-working Military Dad and daycare working Mom. There was no reserve to fall back on.*
>
> *I now look back at that situation and realize such a profound truth. Evil will come in all shapes and sizes, but you **will** survive. Our family did! We prayed that day and gave it to Jesus! 1 Peter 5:8, "Be sober, be vigilant; because your adversary the devil, as a roaring lion, walketh about, seeking whom he may devour;" Satan is on the prowl! He knows your weakness and you better believe He will do all that he can to discourage you and win the battle. This was a very difficult lesson as a young middle school girl when the world revolves around Swatch watches and Girbaud jeans. I learned that when the battles come, and they will, just stop and pray!*
>
> *Most of all realize that 1 Corinthians 15:57, "But thanks be to God, which giveth us the victory through our Lord*

*Jesus Christ." What Satan meant to test, God can use as a testimony. Even if it takes 30 years to learn, I can praise God for the example of Godly parents and the love and the consistency of our Savior. So, from the words of my wise husband, "Your response is your responsibility!"*

I am still in the learning process, but I am proud to say that I am not letting Satan win this battle. I am silencing him with this testimony of my journey. The masquerade is off, but the ball continues on because God is not done with me yet. This is the final entry of a blog that I created called "Knots into Beauty."

*I can remember being in 4-H in elementary school and middle school. No, I was not into the raising cows, sheep, pigs and goats. I was into the cooking and sewing contests. It was neat the opportunities and competitions that I was involved in. I remember one certain time where I was in a cooking contest that was being held at the Pierre Bossier Mall. It was not just one dish, but a themed setting of different things that I had cooked on display. I vaguely remember what I cooked, but I do remember that I had picked Christmas as my theme. For some reason, my Dad was taking me to this contest because my Mom could not. I had a brother and sister that were very active, so they had to divide and conquer many times. I remember my Mom was very organized on the things that I needed to bring and how to set up my display. Poor Dad, I know that he made several trips back and forth from home to the mall just trying to get everything just perfect for me. Dad was determined to have everything that I needed and for me to be happy with my display to show the hard work that Mom and I had put into it. He never quit until it was complete, and I won the contest!*

*I share this story with you because of how many times does Satan throw "knots" in our way to discourage us from the plan that God has set for us. We get distressed, tired, and become defeated. My Dad could have just said "NO!" no more trips back and forth to the house but I probably would have never won if He didn't want it to be just right! Philippians 3:14, "I press toward the mark for the prize of the high calling of God in Christ Jesus." Notice it says PRESS! It means there will be opposition. Keep moving toward the prize!*

*Satan will do all that he can to get you depressed, discouraged and he will make it easy for you to quit. 1 John 4:4, "Ye are of God, little children, and have overcome them: because greater is he that is in you than he that is in the world." The people that are in the world and don't know Jesus belong to Satan already. He won't mess with them, but He wants you to stop being a testimony and witness for Jesus so he will work hardest on you! Just know that Christ has already overcome!*

*So, don't let the "KNOTS" in life stop you from accomplishing God's will. Genesis 50:20, "But as for you, ye thought evil against me; but God meant it unto good..." Jesus was crucified but it didn't stop there. Philippians 3:10, "That I may know him, and the power of his resurrection..." We may not know the outcome during the "knot", but God does! You might just win First Prize!*

Grace is an amazing thing. Allowing ourselves the grace to fail is beautiful, and a process. Understanding that Jesus is the only perfect one and that no matter how hard I try I will make mistakes, falter and mess up but they are not fatal. It is a learning tool. The issue becomes taking personal responsibility for them and realizing what went wrong and why. It takes honesty and reflection within. Wearing a masquerade is deceiving others and ourselves. It robs the world of you- so take it off and give yourself some grace to be human.

# 10

## God Didn't Create Masks, So Be Bold!

Wearing the masquerade allowed me to hide from the truth. The truth that I knew as a Christian and sometimes plain old common sense. I had worn it for so many years that the basic rationale of what was considered normal was skewed with my emotional, physical, and spiritual issues. We all ask, "What is normal?" Normal is relative to the individual, but fact is fact. There is no wavering from it and to do so while deceiving ourselves of the undeniable outcome that will result from it is just another layer of denial. This strengthens the layers of the masquerade.

It all starts with the basics and there is no better fact, truth, or beginning than the Bible. Down through history plaguing our society has been the use and abuse of recreational mind-altering substances. Many people that use these substances have given in to temptation and bought into lies. They are searching for a euphoric feeling and numbing effect that they've been told it could bring. The long-term effects of taking these substances are not realized or just ignored. Many doctors fail to divulge the entire truth about medication to patients, at least mine never did. Anything; whether alcohol, street drugs, recreational drug usage, or even prescription medications that alter the mind, can cause you to err in vision and judgment.

Lack of judgment started way back in the beginning in the Garden of Eden. "And the serpent said unto the woman, Ye shall not surely die; For God doth know that in the day ye eat thereof, then your eyes shall be open, and ye shall be as gods, knowing good and evil.' (Genesis 3:4,5) Satan tempted Adam and Eve to partake of the forbidden fruit that they knew they were told not to have, and he still uses the same tactics on us today. When a person's mind or judgment is impaired in any way shape or form with any kind of substance, it can lead to poor judgment and choices. It can hinder the purity of peace and leading of God. Being sober minded is essential in a Christian's life.

Society can be very accepting of most things because these vices are not all illegal. A new standard and compromise have been accepted in exchange for Biblical promises and truths. The view and opinions of doctors have taken precedence over the view and commandment of our Lord. We have limited God to certain areas in our lives outside of the emotional and mental realm of health. We have placed Him in a box to heal and work only within those confines within the designated perimeters.

I have found from my personal experience, that any substance that alters the mind can change the chemical receptors in the brain and further obstruct underlying problems. In many cases, these substances impair our normal judgment whether physically or spiritually. After any length of time, more whether in strength or number, is needed to numb the pain as the body becomes tolerant and immune. The snowball, or piggyback, effect then occurs of adding drugs on top of drugs. Each drug has its own set of side effects. Haven't you heard any of the commercials on television advertising the new prescriptions with the two to three-minute list of "possible" side effects? Now those side effects require more medication, so you end up taking medicine for the original issue and something else for the side effects themselves.

This explains how I got to the astronomical amount of taking **21** pills a day. It was never my intention, nor did I set out to reach that many prescriptions for that long period of time. I did not intentionally want to max out the allowable dosage of each prescription that I was taking and eventually become addicted. An addict never intentionally chooses at the beginning to become addicted. At first, it is usually an innocent social coping mechanism that they are using to fulfill themselves. They want to chill, numb the pain, or just take the edge off. Unfortunately, before they know it, their body is craving the substance. It becomes a requirement to just function daily.

The prescription drugs that are often used for emotional issues are categorized as depressants, or stimulants, and sometimes both. They are designed to help one feel good, to feel better, or to do better. Those are all fleshly desires that Adam desired in the garden. It was not the actual fruit that Adam desired it was the effect. He was told that it would do for him what he desired. This need can develop into a level of self-worship and self-reliance by refusing to recognize God and his power, love, and authority over our lives.

Many times, prescription medications are used to cope with the physical and emotional pain in our lives. In some cases, not all, this can be considered a direct contradiction to the core values of who God is and what he can do. We will sing the hymns and songs with our mouths proclaiming to the mountain tops that our God reigns, yet we deny in our own hearts, the belief and dependence on Him for our daily emotional functioning.

Some psychological philosophies today take away any responsibility of the patient for their treatment plan. A diagnosis and label can be placed on a person taking away that individual's own personal accountability for wellness. It becomes something we are born with, a gene that is defective, family history, or just society itself. Many of these do factor in our emotions and views of life and experiences, but the complete thought of making our own daily choices is taken away. Many are told that they can't help their position, actions, and reactions; therefore, no liability or responsibility is placed on them as the patient. It is all the disease or condition. Believing this way, now takes the obligation, responsibility, or accountability off someone trying to do anything on their own to get better. Most diagnoses dealing with psychiatric and psychological issues are based solely on the patient's own personal testimony. The doctor's opinion, words, labels, and diagnosis become fact in our lives and our Great Physician's words become null and void.

The rationalization that taking the substance is acceptable because it is a legal prescription from a doctor becomes our persuasive thought. Doctors are not questioned by the average person and the complete reliance upon their judgment is taken. Many of them do not take Biblical principles into consideration for diagnosing and treating patients. We are three parts in nature- body, soul, and spirit or in other words, physical, mental and spiritual. Many times, two of the three are not even taken into consideration. The physical body is treated and that is it. It is not a new thing or fad that the emotional and spiritual are ignored. Even in Biblical times, there were struggles. "And Asa in the thirty and ninth year of his reign was diseased in his feet until his disease was exceeding great; yet in his disease, he sought NOT the Lord, but to the physicians." (2 Chronicles 16:12). Who or what are you seeking first?

After tragic events prescriptions are given with complete legitimacy. The problem and issue arise when month after month a refill is given when the body has become completely dependent on it. The patient now physically requires it and further complications, other than emotional issues arise. Furthermore, coping emotionally is not even addressed. A prescription should not be just written and given without other recommendations for counseling.

Many are finding comfort in a pill instead of finding everlasting comfort in the Great Comforter. "Now our Lord Jesus Christ himself, and God, even our Father, which hath loved us, and hath given us everlasting consolation and good hope through grace, comfort your hearts, and stablish you in every good word and work." (2 Thessalonians 2:16-17) The dependence on the prescriptions then becomes a physical and spiritual issue in nature. The body needs it and the faith in the drug is now substituted for our faith in God.

**Let me be clear right here, that I am not opposed to prescription medication and I will say that with every breath and truly believe in my heart.** I do not want to be misunderstood. I am against the <u>overuse</u> of medications. I am against being diagnosed or labeled with having a disease, disorder, or condition and living out that label never taking into consideration the all-sufficient grace and healing of our Lord. I am against the dependence of taking a "happy pill" instead of getting down to the root of the unhappiness and allowing the joy of the Lord to be our strength. I am against Christians taking medications to fix the emotions and never doing anything to fix the spiritual man. Many times, the Lord or His word are not even sought after for guidance and help.

A Christian needs to realize no matter the season in life, the trial that is going on, or the condition of their circumstances, that Isaiah 51:1 tells us "Hearken to me, ye that follow after righteousness, ye that seek the Lord: look unto the rock whence ye are hewn, and to the hope of the pit whence ye are digged." No matter the rock or mountain in front of you or how deep the pit is, the Lord should be exalted, not a medication. As a child of God, you have Heaven above you, Jesus for you and the Holy Spirit in you that are all strengthening, loving, supporting and rooting for you. Tap into that power first before turning to something else.

Let's backtrack for a moment, on February 13, 1997, Jason and I were up visiting mutual friends in Mountain View, Arkansas. I had grown up in church with these friends for most of my life and so we knew each other's own spiritual backgrounds. We all "knew" that we had all accepted Christ as our personal Savior when we were younger. We had all had been sitting under the teaching and preaching literally since the moment we came out of the womb. This one friend had stated that she had come to the realization that she was never saved when we were younger and recently accepted Christ as her personal Savior. That statement, that night, got me to examining my own salvation. How could I have never truly had my own personal relationship with Christ? I was raised in church and was even teaching a Sunday School class. So surely, I must be confused?

The next morning, I was in a really awful mood. I think Jason was reconsidering our relationship with my unfavorable attitude that morning. We had planned to go to the outdoor amphitheater in town and just bask at the beauty of God's creation. So, as we traveled there my attitude got worse and my emotions were getting the best of me. We sat down on the cold concrete bleachers. He was trying to be so nice and patient with me, but I couldn't contain myself and blurted out like a balloon about to pop, "I think I am lost!"

"What?" He responded with disbelief. See God had used that conversation the night before to cause me to examine my own heart and come to the realization that I had gone through the motions my entire life. I had a head knowledge of what a relationship with Jesus was supposed to be about, but not a personal heart knowledge of Him as my Savior. I had never personally and truthfully asked Jesus Christ to come into my heart and be my Savior and so I did that day!

You may be asking yourself what all this has to do with my journey with mental issues. That night before, when I couldn't sleep, Jason prayed before he went to bed. He asked for God to allow him to witness and to share the gospel with someone the next day! He prayed that prayer with boldness never realizing that he knew very few people in this entire town. Yet, He boldly with faith, courage, and conviction went to the throne with a specific desire never really knowing that the one person that he was going to be able to lead to Christ was going to be me. I was the answered prayer as I accepted Christ as my personal Savior that next day.

Many times, we pray with vagueness and so nonchalantly. We don't comprehend that the petitions that we are offering up are being spoken to our Creator. The fact that we are not specific in our prayer lives can be a lack of faith or a lack of courage. Perhaps we might be afraid that our prayers might actually be answered. I prayed for healing and for the bipolar to just go away out of desperation and a burning desire for it to just all be over. God answered my prayer far better than anything I had desired or prayed for and the diagnosis was completely gone and erased from my own personal medical history. I finally took the spiritual aspect of who I was as a true factor in being whole.

We serve a God that states in Luke 12:7, "But even the hairs on your head are numbered." To me, that means that He is a God of specifics. Thinking about something, wanting, wishing or even needing, is not the same as praying for it. I wanted to be made whole, I wished to be normal, I thought of ways to help myself, but I never truly prayed for the cycle to end. I took man's definition of who I was and was going to be over God's. He created me and he knew me, but I needed to come to him with my desires.

First, and most importantly, is praying for salvation. It is *the* most important and crucial decision that you will ever make in your life. Literally, the difference in your eternity counts on it. The first step is to make yourself stop and to examine yourself inwardly. As I have quoted before in 1 Samuel 16:7 states, "But the LORD said unto Samuel, Look not on his countenance, or on the height of his stature; because I have refused him: for the LORD seeth not as man seeth; for man looketh on the outward appearance, but the LORD looketh on the heart." It is realizing that God does not look at you from the outside. It doesn't matter what masquerade you are wearing, nor how long you have had it on. It doesn't matter if you think you are fooling everyone around you and doing a great job of it. God sees through it and sees your heart. He made you, and he knows you, and no matter what you may cover up so others can't know, he sees right through it.

We all must make the bold decision in our lives to get real and honest. We must get real with ourselves and to be real with God. Praying to God as Psalms 139:23 states, "Search me; O God, and know my heart; try me and know my thoughts." That's a hard prayer to pray and uncomfortable to ask from our Creator. It's asking God to look into those deep dark corners of our hearts and to expose them. Exposing them is the only way to take the next step.

That next step is examining if you have ever accepted Jesus Christ as your Savior. Can you go back to a place, not necessarily a specific date, time, or location? I am talking about an occasion where you repented of your sins and asked Jesus Christ to save you and to come into your life? Have you realized that you will stand before God one day, after you have left this earthly life, and you will be asked why you should be allowed into Heaven? The one and only answer is that you have accepted the perfect sacrifice for your sins and what Jesus did on the cross by shedding his blood for YOU!

Romans 3:23 tells us, "For all have sinned and come short of the glory of God." We each must come to the realization in our own lives that we have sinned. As a society, we categorize sin as big and little, public and private, pet sins and lifestyles. Sin is sin! Sin is anything you do contrary to the perfectness of God and his character. There is only one person that had walked on Earth and lived up to that perfection, and His name is Jesus.

So many will use the excuse "so what's the point? I will never match up to that so why even try?" The point is found in Romans 5:8, "But God commendeth his love toward us and that while we were yet sinners, Christ died for us." Jesus left the beauty, majesty, and perfection of Heaven to come and vail himself in human flesh and suffer as a man.

"Even as the Son of man came not to be ministered unto, but to minister, and to give his life a ransom for many." (Matthew 20:28) So, not only did he know that he had an awful end in sight, but instead of being selfish like many of us would have been, Jesus took every moment to love others and to prepare them to take up the torch and to tell others. "Now before the feast of the passover, when Jesus knew that his hour was come that he should depart out of this world unto the Father, having loved his own which were in the world, he loved them unto the end." (John 13:1). He loved people. He loved limitlessly to every kind, race, status or even with the sins that they had committed, all the way to his dying moments while he was hanging on the cross and in some of his last spoken words. "Then said Jesus, Father forgive them; for they know not what they do." (Luke 23:34a)

So, realizing and admitting that you are a sinner and need a Savior is the beginning, but what is next? Romans 6:23 tells us "For the wages of sin is death; but the gift of God is eternal life through Jesus Christ our Lord." Who doesn't love a gift? Realizing why that gift had to be given is the key. I don't like to do things for free. I like to be paid for the effort and work that I put in. That is in direct contradiction to the definition of a servant. It doesn't have to always be a monetary payment. A simple "thank you" or the satisfaction of the event or project that I was working on which is now complete is enough for me. However, there is a great feeling when you have done something, and you reap the reward for it.

On the flip side of that, is the reward or payment for your sin, which is death. Our sin cannot enter the presence of God in Heaven with His perfection. No matter how many good things in this life that I may do, I will always fail or fall short at something. I will always mess up and so will you. It may be little in our eyes or huge in the public's opinion of acceptable and unacceptable, but it is sin. If there was only one thing that we ever did wrong in our lifetime then that one speck of taintedness is enough to keep us from going to Heaven. We all know that we have done more than one wrong thing in our lives. So, what can we do about it? Keep reading that verse Romans 6:23 and see that it didn't end and is not hopeless, rather, it's full of hope.

"But," that small conjunction in the Bible again, "the gift of God is eternal life through Jesus Christ our Lord." Jesus did it all. So, the question now remains how do you receive this free gift offered to you? Romans 10: 9-10 tells us, "That if thou shalt confess with thy mouth the Lord Jesus, and shalt believe in thine heart that God hath raised him from the dead, thou shalt be saved. For with the heart man believeth unto righteousness; and with the mouth confession is made unto salvation." You pray. You talk to God as if you would talk to your best friend. You admit to him that you know that you need a Savior and admit that your sin has separated you from him. You believe and accept what Jesus did on the cross for you and you want him to come into your heart and into your life by surrendering all that you are to God.

What is next? You "know that you know that you know" and never have to worry or doubt that He will answer your prayer. Romans 10:13 gives us security. "For whosoever shall call upon the name of the Lord shall be saved." It says shall. That is a definitive verb. There is no mistaking it and He will not refuse you. God does not lie and is not the author of confusion, so if he says it and promises it, then he will do it. Once you pray that prayer for salvation with all belief and sincerity in your heart, it is done.

Maybe you have examined your heart and have settled the fact that you have accepted Christ as your personal Savior, the next step is to ask him to evaluate your heart. Request for his guidance and leadership to reveal your struggles and your weaknesses. Pray for direction and discernment in the revelation of both. Knowing that we all have things in our lives that we hide behind, and sometimes that is even our own self-made masks, we need to stop denying that we have struggles and weaknesses. Denial will never help us to strengthen or overcome them.

My denial of the fact that I had issues with medications only made me justify my problem and convince myself otherwise; therefore, never getting real help. Satan will plant any seeds of denial, self-justification, and rationale so that you will condone your actions. You can choose to compromise truth and believe his lies or choose not to.

As I mentioned previously, the Bible tells us "the devil, as a roaring lion, walketh about, seeking whom he may devour;" (1 Peter 5:8). So, he will use any means or tactic to do just that. Deceit and lies both inwardly and outwardly are manipulations that he will conjure up and consistently throw at us to keep us preoccupied. As long as he can keep us focused on everything else, but the truth, he thinks he is winning but that verse never says that he will succeed. It states that he is "seeking whom he may devour." That is not definitive because God is consistently urging, pulling and convicting you to the truth.

Many believe that it's the big issues that we battle out in the big, bad, dark world. The external sins and struggles in life are often the apparent things that we are aware of and stay away from, but internal warfare is the strongest and hardest things we battle. "...purify your hearts, ye double minded." (James 4:8b)

One of those things that we conveniently overlook is Psalms 46:10a "...be still and know that I am God..." Stopping to be still and to listen to God's voice. Many times, we stay so busy because it is easier than being alone with our own heart and thoughts; therefore, it's easier not to hear the voice of God. Hearing his voice requires admitting wrongdoing then that means responsibility. Responsibility means accountability which requires action and change. We take on the attitude if it ain't broke don't fix it, but "If I have walked with vanity, or if my foot hath hasted to deceit; Let me be weighed in an even balance, that God may know mine integrity." (Job 31: 3-4) We need to be honest with ourselves about our own heart and admit to ourselves, and to the Lord, whatever our weakness, pet sin, or our private life may be, that is contrary to God. We need to ask to be forgiven and strengthened.

Living behind the mask for so many years didn't make me a bad person nor did the dependence on medicines, but it did make me immune. Immune to the leading of the Holy Spirit. It did make me numb.

When your foot falls asleep and starts tingling and becoming numb at first it is just that, it is numb and asleep. In a matter of minutes, and sometimes seconds, if you don't start to move it, the circulation starts slowing down. The needle sensation comes and then the pain sets in. It is intense and can be excruciating. It then affects your ability to stand up and even walk. You must shake, jolt, massage or do whatever is necessary to make the feeling come back to life.

Being in denial and numb to our own heart and spiritual condition is much the same way. At first, we think it is no big deal, we realize the Holy Spirit is convicting with the still small voice, we know we are sinning and that we are not in a right relationship with God, yet we ignore it. We shove that still small voice and inner knowing down deep inside. We will sometimes acknowledge that he is there but maybe for another time or concluding that you are fine on your own right now. At that exact moment, it may not seem critical or life changing to you, but it is God our Creator talking personally to you.

Ignoring the conviction and leading becomes easier each time we choose to dismiss it and suppress the Holy Spirit. The more this becomes a habit and ritual the easier our hearts become hardened, immune and less aware of reality and spiritual matters. It becomes numb and even though on the outside we may look like we have it all together and functioning just fine, the inside can become cold and calloused. Over time that numb heart will begin to tingle with an inward pain and hurt, and that hurt heart will start pouring out in all areas of our lives. Many times, the pain will then cause us to project our unhappiness onto others. It will cause our walk with Christ to become stagnant and will paralyze our usefulness for him and who he intended each of us to be.

Many will think and testify that it will never happen to that extreme or just rationalize behaviors with some other reasoning or justification that they are "not that bad off." They proclaim that they will never allow their relationship with God to become that divided and fractured. They defend their actions to themselves and others by believing the facts that they are a Christian, they go to church, and they give and serve others, so things can't be as bad off as I am describing.

So, did I! I was not an evil person doing sins out in the world to destroy others or the church. Mine was a battle that was destroying me from the inside and spilling outward onto my relationships with the ones closest to me of whom God blessed me with. It was all because of the masquerade that I was wearing in the ball I called "my life".

I was a Christian, a preacher's wife, a mother, a Sunday school teacher, a youth group worker, and a daycare worker and all the while I was playing a role as a double agent. I was acting. The real me was too hard to bear. Admitting my frailty would require action and dependence on something or someone else other than myself including God. That would require an acknowledgement that I wasn't in real control and that I was not perfect. I couldn't bring myself to confess that, much less have anyone else find that out about me. Oh, it was easy to not outwardly proclaim with an egotistical attitude that I was perfect and in complete control of my life because I knew better and knew what I was supposed to say and portray. Acting *became* easy.

Praying boldly and specifically for God to show you what area in your life that you need him to take control is the only answer to be whole.

Whether it be first realizing that you never have accepted him as your Lord and personal Savior, or maybe you live a double life. Maybe you are one person at church then someone else at home or maybe, just maybe, you are living a lie with a double personality lying to yourself. Maybe you are someone on the outside and a completely different individual on the inside.

Maybe your mask has gotten so familiar, or the voice of Satan and his lies are continually speaking in your life, you have begun to believe them. The familiarity is there, and you no longer recognize the voice of God. That was what I had become to believe as truth and how I was so beat down for many years never realizing it and certainly not looking for rescuing. Pray boldly right now for God to examine you, expose the true condition of your heart and the lies of Satan and to exalt you to be who God created you to be.

I prayed for many years that God would heal me. I prayed that the stigma, the struggle and the situations in my life would change being a bipolar patient. I wanted the depression gone, the anxiety quieted, the internal war between my mind and my heart to sign a peace treaty. I wanted the diagnosis to be erased and forgotten like a bad dream. I prayed and I prayed, and I prayed more out of desperation than belief, but I prayed anyway. I prayed fervently and continually, but I was praying for my own selfish agenda. With the persistence of my praying, I finally realized the need behind the need. The true condition of where I was and where I was headed. My prayers changed as the true need was exposed. Sometimes God doesn't change the situation, but he does change us.

But now I understand what Psalms 37:4 really meant. "Delight thyself also in the Lord: and he shall give thee the desires of thine heart." I had to learn to find contentment, gladness, gratification, and satisfaction in one person and one person only and that was Jesus. I didn't learn that lesson until I was stripped of everything in my life, sitting in a psychiatric ward literally scared for my life. That is when I found myself at the foot of Jesus' feet looking up. When I turned my attention off myself and I placed it on him, my prayer for healing was answered.

Searching for answers, peace, happiness, and love in anything or anyone other than Jesus will only leave you disappointed, frustrated and empty. Being bold and truly honest with God and most importantly yourself is where you need to start. That boldness and pure unfiltered truth will open up your heart. Those deep desires that you had only wished and dreamed about will evolve into new ones by your Creator or they will change from your wishes, your dreams, your desires to His.

Taking off the mask to be able to pray boldly as Cindy and not as anyone else is freeing. God sees through the "supposed to be" person, the "title" or the hats that you wear because He created you. He knows what and who is hiding behind the layers and that is who he wants to come to him. Lay all the masks down and come as you are to God and you will be amazed, like I am, of all the places you will go and the blessings in store for the life that he intends for you to have. It will be a ball discovering it all!

# 11

## Blinded by the Masquerade

Pin the tail on the donkey is a great childhood game where a person wears a blindfold or closes their eyes. The goal of the game is to try and strategically place the picture or object on the proper place all the while not being able to see. It is often so funny after the object is placed and the blindfold is taken off, to see how far away from the intended mark you missed putting it. Usually, everyone bursts out in giggles or makes excuses why they were so far from the target. The logic behind being blindfolded is to obstruct your vision. It is to make you unaware of what you are doing, but still requesting you to act as if you can see. That is exactly just how Satan works in our lives.

John 10:10 clearly warns us, "The thief cometh not, but for to steal, and to kill, and to destroy: I am come that they might have life, and that they might have it more abundantly." We need to realize that Satan will come. We are warned over and over in the Bible. It is not an "IF" or "MAYBE," it IS a definite. Just like when you get that weather alert on your phone with the annoying beeps and it says tornado watch, you usually just ignore it, but if the words "warning" is used then you pay much closer attention to what is happening around you and the location of the storm.

This is definitely a warning! "For we wrestle not against flesh and blood, but against principalities, against powers, against the rulers of the darkness of this world, against spiritual wickedness in high places." (Ephesians 6:12). We are warned over and over that "... Satan hath desired to have you, that he may sift you as wheat:" (Luke 22:31). Why are we shocked when everything is going just as we want it to and then the bottom fall out when the storm rolls in and begins to rage in our lives?

Crisis in our lives can come and go. Many times, in life they come in and stay for seasons. They stay a lot longer than we ever wanted. We are told plainly in Job 14:1, "Man that is born of a woman is of few days, and full of trouble." We are warned that it will not be easy and not guaranteed for how long we will have to endure. So, taking on the mindset of our family motto that "your response is your responsibility" is the key in dealing with these attacks. Yet, over and over we are shocked, dumbfounded and perhaps all around defeated when the attacks bombard us.

What kinds of things is Satan blinding us with? The biggest issue is usually concerning our spiritual condition. When he can make our hearts all confused, consumed, and conflicted then we are not in a place to be used of our Lord. Confusion over eternity and our spiritual conditions are the biggest lies. What is it, where is it, and how we get there? Confusion, or delusion, that Satan uses is deceiving us into believing that sins are not a big deal.

Satan wants you to be selfish and believe that it is your life, your issues, and your choices. He wants you to think that you are not hurting anyone else so it's none of anyone's business what you do. Satan is lying to you. He has used this tactic from the beginning of time, so why are we so surprised? His ways haven't changed. They aren't new and they aren't anything that we haven't been forewarned about. Yet we are still caught off guard. He constantly brings doubt and questions about the promises and truth of God. In the beginning, in the Garden, he tempted Eve and asked, "Yea, hath God said." (Genesis 3:1). If he used it then and it worked, why change? He just continues to use it over and over. When we are doubting the promises and provisions of God, we need to stop and realize that yes, God did say.

Many contemplate why those who don't have God in their lives seem to flourish, prosper, and be at peace. It appears that the blessings just flow from Heaven right down on them, yet followers suffer. So why would you choose to be one of those to suffer having a life filled with heartache and troubles while following Christ? Matthew 5:45 tells us,

"That ye may be the children of your Father which is in heaven: for he maketh his sun to rise on the evil and on the good, and sendeth rain on the just and on the unjust." Those that don't care about eternal issues are experiencing their "heaven" right now and unfortunately one day that will end if they never accept Christ. Dying without accepting Jesus Christ as your personal Savior means eternal separation from God living in torment in Hell. Those who live for Christ and seem to be bombarded with trial after trial and never really seem to appear to have peace will get to enjoy that everlasting peace for ALL of eternity. I am thankful I chose temporary trials for eternal peace, have you?

If you do struggle with mental health issues, Satan can use that to confuse and defeat you. Let me be very clear with this, I am NOT a medical health professional, nor do I claim to be. I am an advocate for balance. There are truly legitimate mental health issues where chemicals are not functioning properly in the brain. Also, some experience hormone imbalances that do cause anxiety and/or depression. There is circumstantial depression, or post-traumatic stress disorder, that people can suffer from when tragedy happens. This can occur as a result of a loss or having experienced a tragedy in their lives. I, once again, am stating plainly and clearly that I am not against medicine. I am against the overuse of medicine and not using the coping skills our Heavenly Father wants us to learn and use to deal with life and the issues within it. There is nothing "cookie cutter" about mental health and I can only share from my own personal experience what went wrong and brought me to the point where I am today and what I have learned from it all.

I personally wanted medicine to fix me. I wanted all the depression, sadness, loss and grief to go away and when it didn't the anxiety of struggling with those feelings settled in. I am against the unrealistic idea that medicine is supposed to fix you and that taking a pill is the "end all be all" and only answer when coping with life and the stresses of it. I am against solely depending on a pill and not relying on our Lord and Savior who created life. I am against the overuse of medications, the addiction to medication and trusting doctors more than we trust the Great Physician. I am against labeling each person in an attempt to diagnosis someone because God is who created you and the only one who can define you. Fitting someone into a category or a number on an insurance code or pharmaceutical company form only leads to more struggles if it is not accurate. I am against someone not putting in the hard work of Bible study, prayer, counseling, and behavior modification techniques and solely running to medication as the first and only choice for treatment.

But most of all, I am against being silent. Silent because of the stigma and embarrassment that our society and churches put on mental health issues whether it be depression, anxiety, all the above, or something completely different. When I went into the hospital the first time and by no fault of my husband, it was just explained to the church that I was just getting some help. No one in my church knew the magnitude of my mental state, and even as many of you have read these lines in this book you are probably shocked by the years of covering up that occurred for the sake of saving my family from embarrassment.

That only caused me to keep my secret more of a secret and hidden. It allowed my masquerade to stay neatly and permanently fixed in place. It didn't force me to be accountable for my actions. Satan used that to make me oblivious to reality and convinced me into believing that things were not as bad off as they really were. That's how he operates, camouflaging things in our lives to convince us that things, including us and our actions, aren't that bad or we can handle it all on our own. That is just what I allowed him to do for too many years in my life. Those emotions would continue escalating in my life and I could not get any peace. All our fears, hurts, struggles and stresses need to be taken to the throne of our Heavenly Father and laid at His feet.

The spiral downward doesn't usually happen all at once but a little bit at a time over a period of time. It happens while we are being distracted and deceived by Satan. That is how a person, like me, got to the point of taking 21 pills a day. I was looking for a cure and it wasn't being found. I wanted to be well but was looking in all the wrong places finding no true and lasting real solutions. Satan had fooled me into thinking I needed just the right combination of medicines to be well.

Those small negative feelings and whispers in my mind at the beginning began to intensify as I began to believe Satan. Yes, I said feelings. Feelings are NOT real. They change with each circumstance and situation, but God is real, and the promises of His word are truth and fact. 1 Corinthians 14:33 clearly states, "For God is not the author of confusion, but of peace, as in all churches of the saints." Down in my heart, the Holy Spirit was telling me one thing, but Satan was telling me something completely different.

I should have realized from the beginning why I was struggling. IT WAS SATAN! He is looking to devalue, confuse, and devour you. He wants the you that God created you to be to be obsolete. Realize where those negative feelings are coming from and get in the Bible and arm yourself with the truth. Realize the truth behind the masks and lies of who you are, what truth is and what you are created to do.

For those of you who may have been given a mental health diagnosis, it is okay. There is no shame in what you can't fix. But do know that even though the chemistry in your brain or the hormonal imbalance in your endocrine system may not function as it was created to do, your heart which is the seat of your emotions can. It can be at peace during the storm. You can find peace in the middle of a crisis and you can find strength when fear sets in. Those are not chemical matters they are often spiritual ones.

Satan will use confuse your heart and convince you into thinking that you can get serious about God and spiritual matters later and that it doesn't have a factor in your mental health. Remember Satan is a thief. He is wanting to rob you of genuine peace and spending eternity with Jesus. He wants to rob you of time. As long as you are down and defeated you are wasting precious time. Satan will keep you in turmoil inwardly, so you are useless outwardly, all the while, also keeping your world in chaos and keeping you paralyzed and hiding behind the masquerade that he created.

A busy schedule, financial issues, and health problems are all factors that can contribute to being overwhelmed. It can be relentless and feel hopeless to a point of no relief. If Satan can keep you distracted by so many other things your focus will not be on the one beneficial thing. If your calendar is so full that you don't have time for the one who created you and keeps oxygen pumping thru your lungs, then you are too busy. Remember that just as you think that things are going the way that you want them, and you can breathe again with relief then get ready. You better brace yourself because Satan is waiting to pounce.

The Bible clearly tells us to "Be still and know.." See, we often reference that verse and stop just at those four words. We need to look at it in its entirety. Psalms 46:10 "Be still, and know that I am God: I will be exalted among the heathen, I will be exalted in the earth." Be still means to stop everything you are doing and just breathe. That does not imply just being physically still like we often think. In our car, focused and distracted by traffic, is only being physically still not mentally and emotionally. It literally means the complete absence of motion. It means to be calm and tranquil. To many of us moms, that sounds like a perfect vacation. Imagine yourself in your happy place. To you, it may be at the ocean just listening to the waves or on the fishing lake just listening to the crickets and bullfrogs as they croak.

Learning to quiet your schedule and calendar and making time to be alone with our Lord is so very important. Jesus himself went away from the crowd and it tells us just that in James 5:16, "And he withdrew himself into the wilderness and prayed." So, realizing that your schedule is too cluttered to allow time with Christ is a step in the right direction. Knowing that Satan wants you blinded and preoccupied with busyness will allow you to stop from the rat race and look inwardly to examine your heart and the condition of it.

Don't be so consumed with your own performance of good deeds that you forget the most important factor. The next part of the verse is that He is God. You need to learn to remain silent and still to bask in the love and goodness of who God really is. Stop strictly talking to Him and learn to listen for him.

Many times, we equate busyness with holiness. I grew up thinking if I was active in church, never missed a service and was always good that God loved me more. I lived out the equation of performance love verses perfect love. This journal writing from January 7, 2002, proves that it has been a lifelong struggle and lesson that I am trying to grasp.

> *I have always been one to enjoy being in the spotlight. I will volunteer for things. I always have to be doing something. I need to come to the point in my life where it is not about me, but about Christ in me. If I am the one always doing things, then it is me that they see and not Jesus. That is a sin.*

> *I need to focus more of my time working on me than all the projects. It fills a lot of my time and I lose time for Jesus. I make Him second choice when He should be first. I need to slow down and enjoy the quiet times. Those are the times I can allow Jesus to speak to my heart. With all the clutter in my life, I can't feel his presence.*

James 1:17 tells us that, "Every good and perfect gift is from above.." and Romans 8:39 states, "Nor height, nor depth, nor any other creature, shall be able to separate us from the love of God, which is in Christ Jesus our Lord." So that validates that no matter what I do or don't do it will not make God love me anymore than He does right now or any less. I can't work for His love. I can't work for Him to love me more than my neighbor or for me to be the apple of His eye. I already am!

The most memorized, quoted, and recognized verse of all time, John 3:16 says, "For God so loved the world that he gave his only begotten Son that whosoever believeth in him should not perish but have everlasting life." Now take that verse and make it personal for you. For God so loved (Insert your name here). When I put my name there and realized that he loved me before I was even born, it was eye-opening. He loved me perfectly before I taught one Sunday school lesson, before I cooked one homemade casserole for a fellowship, before I decorated the church for holidays and even before I ever volunteered to do crafts at Vacation Bible School. He loved me before I joined any committees or volunteered for any positions or gave my first offering in the plate. He loves me. He loves Cindy Hebert for just me.

Now do not get me wrong, none of those actions or jobs are bad. I should want to do those things because I love him but not to try and make him love me more. I can't buy his love because I don't have enough money, and surely can't impress him with my talent because hello, he created everything. It doesn't matter, even if I did, because that's not what he desires. All he truly wants is me. My heart completely surrendered and in love with him. Because we strive to have a heart like his, it then gives us the drive to want to do all those things. We should want to share the love that we have received from God with other people so that they can experience it for themselves. But do not mistake being motivated by a performance-driven relationship with God rather than your own personal relationship with him.

Satan also wants to keep us conflicted in every area of our lives. Conflict within on a personal level, and without on a relational level, can place an unbelievable amount of pressure on someone, causing chaos on all levels. Just an example that I personally experienced was to have doctors tell me one thing and others tell me something completely contrary. Then my heart was telling me a third thing completely different from the other two.

How do you ever truly know absolute truth in all of it? People say it is only relevant to the individual, but I am telling you that you must trust God for undeniable concrete truth for yourself. You get off of the internet sites and you stop self-diagnosing. You stop living out the self-fulfilling prophecy of the diagnosis, symptoms, reactions, and labels of everyone else around. Stop listening to their expectations for you.

Be you behind every layer of the masquerade. Live life as God intended for it to be for you. Learn to listen to, and for, the voice of God. You will believe in whatever voice you listen for and to the most. God talks to us through the Holy Spirit. He is that still small voice inside of you, just listen. The cry of the world, and Satan, are going to be constantly bombarding you. "For the Lord your God is he that goeth with you, to fight for you against your enemies, to save you." (Deuteronomy 20:4) Be prepared and guarded and don't let either take seed as reality in your life. You need to believe the truth. John 8:32 states, " And ye shall know the truth, and the truth shall make you free." There is absolute truth for you, and it is God and his word.

The conflict that goes on inside of you is a war. Be prepared and get armed. The conflict outside of you is real because others will not understand total dependence on God. But I would much rather battle in an all-out war with God on my side, then to have any other factor or friend in my corner. Settle in your heart to stop fighting the battle on your own. "The Lord shall fight for you, and ye shall hold your peace." (Exodus 14:14)

I don't know about you, but buying the groceries is not the hard part of shopping, neither is putting them away, it's the carrying them in the house that I hate. Dragging those heavy overstuffed thin plastic bags filled with eggs and spaghetti sauce side by side. You juggle between carrying too many to have fewer trips back and forth, risking dropping that brand-new bottle of sauce in the garage or bumping them into your bread or eggs, or just deciding to make more trips to guarantee the delicate items are safe. It's a load lugging your menu items for the week all balanced in your hands from your vehicle into your home, but you do it because you certainly don't want to waste any of your groceries or money.

We are the exact same way in our lives. We juggle it all trying to balance it by ourselves day in and day out many times dropping things, people or ourselves, only to have it to come shattering to the ground making a mess. That mess can be prevented if we will stop trying to carry the load all by ourselves. "For my yoke is easy, and my burden is light." (Matthew 11:30) Many times we think we are bothering God with our problems, so we don't approach him with our issues. Learn to let the true victor take over in your life. Let him unpack each and every area of your life which such love, gentleness, and ease as if it were eggs or fresh bread, taking the utmost care for who you are and having your best interest in mind.

Personally, the ball that I refer to as my life changed music altogether and became enjoyable when I finally learned to be real, take off the masquerade, and I allowed God to orchestrate the music. The weight of being my own DJ was gone. The beat of trying to please everyone else was no longer necessary. I was no longer preoccupied with the festivities around me or the need to maintain my cover-up and experience the truth of who God truly was and who He created me to be. When I learned to be still and enjoy spending time with my Savior without any barriers or walls of lies and deception, then I could find peace, victory and the sweet fellowship with the one who finally made me masquerade free. I didn't have to hide anymore.

# 12

## You Choose

Bondage is being paralyzed, shackled or bound to something and it inhibits you from moving or going forward. Satan's voice and ideas that he planted had become familiar and the voice of God had become quiet. No, I did not say God left or wasn't there. His voice had become unfamiliar. Satan's lies had taken up residence and shackled me. I was bound!

I lived for many years believing that I was going to live with debilitating depression and anxiety. The biggest issue was that I was believing everything that I was told by the world and many doctors. They had convinced me that medicine was the only way and I had become a slave to the clock waiting for the next round of medicine to be taken. I was confined to a strict schedule that limited my capability to be spontaneous or vary from my routine.

As the years rolled along and the medication kept piling up, the behaviors had become crippling, and my emotions were desensitized. I was in bondage to the lies I had bought into and I was convinced that this is who I was, how things had to be, and no one understood what I was going through. I defended that argument to everyone who challenged me, yet I neatly applied my lipstick on to make sure my smile was just so and my "I've got it all together" mask was put on every single day for others who knew me. If I felt I couldn't control my actions, then why didn't everyone see all of them or why was I able to resist them when necessary?

I was in bondage and completely convinced that there was something wrong with me and that I needed all 21 of the pills. I was motivated to keep searching and taking them and that eventually, I would find the right combination. I had bought into the lie that each outburst, fit of rage, and extreme chaos was a direct result of my diagnosis and that I could not control them. I had become a monster and was scared of myself, with the things that I was doing, and the self-harm that I would think about. I was crying out just like in Psalm 13:1, "How long wilt thou forget me, O Lord: forever? How long wilt thou hide thy face from me?" I was "playing church" with my smile on and my mask neatly in place yet never really having faith and believing that God could and would deliver me. I knew what to say to each audience around me as if I was reciting a well-rehearsed script.

It is no coincidence that recovery meetings and centers are popping up all over our country. Satan has convinced people into thinking that addiction will never happen to them and that they don't really have a problem. One wrongful act can lead to two. It is then the snowball effect and downhill from there. I wholeheartedly believe that no one sets out to become an addict and no one likes to admit it either. Who really wants to feel like they are wearing a scarlet letter of shame or a cloak of guilt to remind them constantly that they are being watched and judged when the truth comes out? Everyone knows the moment that the secret becomes public then people now place you under a microscope. You feel people begin watching you as if they are waiting for you to mess up or slip up.

The bondage of guilt, shame and secrecy can further put your issues into hiding especially in a church setting. That is the one place we should be able to ask for prayer and seek support from other Christian believers. That is the place that should be able to give accountability with love, encouragement and prayer support. Yet, we often look down and shun the people that open their closets up at church and allow all the skeletons to come rolling out when they are asking for help.

I am reminded of one of the first Sunday's we had in our church. A new converted Christian asked for prayer for an addiction that they were battling. It was very raw, open and honest and oh, so beautiful all at the same time. I cried. I cried because at that split moment I thought and was convinced in my heart that this is what church should be about. Truly bearing each other's burdens and seeking help from other believers. The sad, and the beautiful thing is that this person didn't know any better. They had not been skewed by the idea that in a "normal" church setting you would have never heard that. I was a three time a week and sometimes in between attender and I would have never dreamed of asking for prayer for my addiction. Many times, the church just doesn't understand the magnitude of the struggle not only with addiction but also mental health. Our prayer request list becomes a medical report and obituary reading instead of truly bearing one another's burdens or "iron sharpening iron." The minute someone gets real, raw and honest our minds start racing with thoughts like, "Can you believe they did that or said that?" "How did they get caught?" "Just watch, they will do it again."

Satan had convinced Eve that the fruit was not as bad as it seemed, and he still uses that same tactic today. We begin to believe that little pet sins and secrets that we have are contained in the privacy of our own home, or our hearts, and do not affect anyone else. We feel as if it is no one's business what our struggles are so we don't publicize it in the form of prayer needs, or we just say "unspoken." That mind frame will keep you enslaved to secrecy, shame, and self-doubt. It makes you start thinking two steps ahead to make sure your tracks are covered. It makes you deny who you really are and then the masquerade wearing begins and continues so that you not only protect yourself from the outside world but also from your own reality. You either start hiding, continue to hide or go even deeper into the process of staying hidden all the while still struggling.

Many have asked why I completely stopped the 19 pills at one time. I would not advise anyone to do it that way without the watchful eye of their doctor, and I know that there could have been some serious complications in the detoxing phase of my recovery. The side effects of increased anxiety, depression, dizziness, electric shocks, headaches, loss of coordination, spasms, nausea, nightmares, tremors, vomiting, sweating and hallucinations were enough, but I could have had a serious seizure, a heart attack and I could have died. But I felt as if inside I was dead already. I knew me and the only way to get off the medicines because of the depth of the addiction and complete dependence on them on so many different levels was to completely stop them at once. I had to. If I had tried weaning like a few times before, then I personally believe I would have never gotten off them.

My body was not only addicted to medications, but I was addicted to the idea of taking handfuls of pills. It was a ritual, and habit, to swallow several at a time convincing myself it was my lifeline to sanity. It was my bondage and addiction of going to that little brown or white container and unscrewing the lid. Grabbing each and everyone and gulping them down with a glass of water as my daily routine. When I did it there were endorphins that were released almost instantly like a placebo effect. I was of the absolute unwavering opinion that I needed all of them to fix me or to just be able to function on the level that I was. I never thought things would change so the doctor's advising me how to properly stop was what I knew had to be done. It had to be all or nothing by stopping the medications instantly.

The last time that I was in the psychiatric ward was my last experience of feeling like I was in bondage. I had signed a voluntary commit and that requires a minimum stay. I felt as if I was going to be shackled to that hospital for days like my previous stay while my husband was plotting his next action, but it didn't happen. I stayed one night. I walked out of the hospital free on the next morning with my husband. I was not in prison in that hospital nor was I going to stay in prison to the pills, my diagnosis, or my masquerade. That night in the suicide watch cold hospital holding room, "I called upon the Lord in distress: the Lord answered me, and set me in a large place." (Psalms 118:5) He set me free -free from me!

Now do not be naive enough to think that you will escape from any consequences for your actions because I didn't. The Bible clearly teaches us that you will reap from the actions that you choose or have chosen to sow. "Be not deceived; God is not mocked: for whatsoever a man soweth, that shall he also reap." (Galatians 6:7) I have been blessed not to have relationship issues with my family, but I do have physical side effects from the many years of heavy medications. I have some nerve shocks and restless leg issues in both my arms and legs each and every day. As crazy as it may seem, I am thankful. Despite the pain and discomfort, it is a thankful reminder of how far God has brought me. Every time I have a shock, or a night of what I describe as kicking, it allows me to reminisce of the love and grace of God in my life. I rub my essential oils on my arms and legs every night to allow me to sleep calmly and I thank God for the reminder of the way things used to be. Thanking him for setting me free from the bondage that I was chained to for so many years, allowing me to live maskless and now dance freely as me.

Satan wants to convince you that your situation and circumstances will never change. IT CAN! He wants to convince you that your addiction, pet sin, lifestyle or your idol isn't harming anyone. IT IS! Your behavior may not kill you, but it will hurt you physically, emotionally, and spiritually, and will affect those around you. Choose to change with the power of God and accept the grace, forgiveness, and love that he freely offers. Circumstances will never change as long as you keep doing the same thing you are doing. Choose differently, believe differently, try differently. Try life without the mask and with the Lord. Realize it's okay not to be okay but don't stay that way!

I have looked back overtime trying to figure out how things got the way that they did. I wonder how I got so tangled up in the web of lies, defeat, and deception. Do you know how a spider web is translucent? And you don't realize it is there until it hits you smack dab in the middle of your face when you walk into it? The silky yet sticky web is pasted on your skin and the more you pull it in one direction trying to get it off the more it secures itself on the other side. The network of silk is all intertwined together and is hard to remove. We usually have to go and wash off to remove it completely.

That is how Satan works as you allow your weaknesses to dominate you and believe that you have it all under control. Suddenly you walk right into the web of lies and are trapped and no longer recognizable. We are stuck, attached, and in a mess. We need to wash it all off with a fresh start. The cleansing of God can remove the web of your past, the web of lies you believe, and have created for yourself; furthermore, he can wash away the web of desires for whatever addiction or battle you are facing.

As I was preparing to write, I asked many friends much wiser and some even in the medical profession very detailed questions about my medical history trying to understand things. The web that Satan had orchestrated with my doctors to allow me to pick up the phone and just verbally communicate my present situation and needs is not customary. The system that we had created of them advising me over the phone to increase medications or dosages without a face to face visit is not advisable. A complete checkup in order to assess my mental state at that time should have been conducted. This practice and relationship that had been established kept the shackles securely fastened and allowed me to become deeper and deeper in bondage.

I have been told over and over when I share the complete list of medications with those in the health or medical field, that they are shocked that I was ever functioning. It was described to me once as "astounding." I was told that the negative side effects that I was experiencing from many of the prescriptions were probably the reason behind adding more. When medications are prescribed to someone it usually only requires one to be effective. Multiple different types of prescriptions for the same symptom usually aren't needed. Instead of stopping one and trying something else, mine just kept piggybacking on top of each other.

Another factor about my medical journey is that it is not normally medically advised to immediately stop taking any psychiatric medications. The advice is to do a very short and slow process of weaning. Many times, supplements are given to ease the symptoms of the detox. I did experience many of the withdrawal symptoms but nothing so detrimental to my health that I was not able to fully recover. There is absolutely nothing textbook or normal about the ability to do what God has allowed to be done in my life, but I believe God doesn't work in the normal. It is also typical that once someone is on psychotropic medication, they are usually on some form for the rest of their lives. Becoming immune to the medications after prolonged usage is normal but usually, replacement medications are added rather than being taken completely off.

The only explanation for any of the things that occurred in my situation and can even be possible is God. He broke the chains and set me free. "But as for you, ye thought evil against me; but God meant it unto good, to bring to pass, as it is this day, to save much people alive." (Genesis 50:20). See Satan had me bound for years but I now claim John 8:36, "If the Son therefore shall make you free, ye shall be free indeed."

Maybe you are in bondage to the lies someone told you growing up or something awful that has happened to you. Maybe you have never healed from the scars of a relationship gone wrong or a loved one that left too soon. Satan WILL take all the unfortunate circumstances in our lives and begin with just planting that small seed of bitterness, doubt, and anger. It all begins with a slight whisper. Remember again, that's all he had to do to Eve in the garden.

Maybe you look at the bottles of medicines that you are taking and start to think "is this how life has to be?" or "am I doing my part to get well?" Maybe you think the addiction, the fears, grief, anxiety, or bitterness are just too heavy and too far gone and you don't even know where to start to be whole again. Maybe you justify your depression or anxiety because of the things that you have endured in this life which leads to heavy doses of medications or addictions to form in your life. You CAN be free!

You start with deciding. It will not be easy or fun or desirable, but you start with wanting more for your life. You take it one moment at a time making bold Godly choices. You realize each step forward is important and do not give yourself the option to quit rather to press on. If you quit trying, then you will be right back to where you started, and you will regret it. Then you will place even more guilt on yourself for not seeing it though. So, choose to not let the ball stop and choose to dance on to a different tune without a mask this time. Be who God created you to be before the clouded view came in and took your joy.

Maybe you struggle with insecurity and it pokes a hole in your heart. Your insecurity that you hide behind has become your masquerade. Realize that it is not bigger than your Savior. The consumption of everything you aren't needs to recognize everything you are, and you need to pinpoint who is keeping you defeated-Satan. He's consuming your time with all the negative thoughts of who you aren't so you can't do for God and be who you are. You need to shift the hypersensitivity that you have for yourself and be in tune with the sensitivity of the Spirit. That is where the truth lies, and confidence is gained.

It is all about who God created us to be and wants us to become. "Trust in the LORD with all thine heart; and lean not unto thine own understanding." (Proverbs 3:5) It is not just about what we know and can see but what our Creator knows and sees in the big picture of things. He is always faithful even if we are not. We are reminded in Deuteronomy 31:8, "And the Lord, he is that doth go before thee; he will be with thee, he will not fail thee, neither forsake thee, fear not, neither be dismayed."

Do not miss the blessings around you while wishing for something else. Your blessings outweigh your burden and the present situation that you are going through. "For I reckon that the sufferings of this present time are not worthy to be compared with the glory which shall be revealed in us." (Romans 8:18) His grace far outweighs any shame, hurt or heartache that we may experience in this life. So be passionate about the present and press forward while your pain turns into praise and you have the strength to persevere for the future. Just look around you and realize that someone else is praying for what you have.

Redirect your focus and place it in the hands of the most powerful and your pain will turn into praise. You must seek Him. (Deuteronomy 4:29) "But if from thence thou shalt seek the LORD thy God, thou shalt find him, if thou seek him with all thy heart and with all thy soul." Sincerely seek Him, don't look at him like he is a genie in a bottle that wants to grant you three wishes when you touch it. Seek with all your heart in devoted prayer and Bible study. It's not just a thought or mind process but it's also an active process of spending devoted time with Him.

You must also stand firm in the security that we have in our Savior no matter what the day may throw at you. You must decide to believe that "This is the day which the LORD hath made; we will rejoice and be glad in it." (Psalms 118:24) Realizing that happiness is not determined by things in this world but your relationship with the One who created all things. We were warned over and over that, "Man that is born of a woman is of few days, and full of trouble." (Job 14:1) Push away from all the negativity in your life and go praise God because of the positive. Change your heart to seek His heart. The hardships may not lessen but the load and your perspective sure will with Jesus. The wrong can be made right in our lives.

To trust God in the good times and when the light is shining bright is not hard to do, but it is learning to trust Him in the dark that seems impossible. You must have faith. "Now faith is the substance of things hoped for, the evidence of things not seen." (Hebrews 11:1) Don't continue to live in sackcloth and ashes giving yourself the okay to stay where you are. Don't just accept that you will stay all depressed forever, that you will never be free from anxiety, or that the addiction is too strong. Stop thinking over and over about how bad of a person you have become or that life will never be "normal." Get up and choose to try to learn to live as a flame, and shine, because that is what you were created to do. "For thou wilt light my candle: the LORD my God will enlighten my darkness." (Psalm 18:28) Your darkness will not be lit by your willpower or strength, but by him.

Place your hand over your heart. Feel it beating? That is purpose. Maybe you have tried over and over and over again, and everyone has given up on you ever getting well or right. Maybe you are so down in the pit that the light is now foreign to you and even if you did see it would hurt your eyes. I am telling you to try one more time. That one more time might just be your last time of failing, but you won't know until you try.

Fight with every ounce of who you are because the hardest part is convincing your mind what you are doing is right. The heart is usually in it. It is the mind that you must convince. The longest distance in the world is the eighteen inches from the head to the heart. Trust the Lord that resides in your heart because Satan can't live in there if you are God's child, but he will try and wreak havoc in your mind. Every spiritual battle can be won or lost in the threshold of the mind.

Don't answer the door when the enemy knocks. Recognize Satan's lies quickly and replace them with truth. The devil will give up when he sees you are not going to give in. You can't live a positive life maintaining a negative mind. Whether it is a shout from the mountain top or a tear streaming down your face- surrender it all to God. He knows and hears, but he doesn't just stop there, He loves and answers too.

The great news is my story didn't end without a family and in a psychiatric ward and yours does not have to end either. Just because you have been shackled, defeated or hiding for a long time, or the hurt is so deep that the pit has become your home, God wants to break those chains of bondage and set you free. He not only wants to deliver you FROM something but deliver you TO something. He wants you to take off your masquerade and to be you, the one whom he created and the one whom he loves.

Freedom is a precious gift, but it is not really free. The freedom recipient gets to enjoy it because the Giver already made the sacrifice. Is it really free since it comes at a price? We can live in freedom of death, hell, and the grave because of what Christ did at Calvary but we can also live free from the shackles of sin, hurt, addictions, and our past because of Christ.

Let's look at the story of Lazarus in John chapter 11. Martha and Mary had given up on Jesus coming. In verse 19 it states that they were being comforted. They were grieving. They had given up hope. You may be there today in your situation or be affected by someone else's actions and you did all that you could to get them help. Just like Martha and Mary, they tried to get Jesus to come on their timetable to heal Lazarus. They did all they knew to do and still were not getting the results that they wanted when they wanted it.

Martha was grieving and upset and she even blamed Jesus. In verse 21, "...Lord, if thou hadst been here, my brother had not died." It is so easy to play the blame game on yourself or someone else why things are the way that they are. Then Mary stating in verse 32, "...Lord, if thou hadst been here, my brother had not died." Sometimes our problems are a direct result of someone else's actions and sometimes they are our own. Things happen in life beyond our mental capacity of understanding for no apparent rhyme or reason. We don't understand them or why they happen. We can't comprehend them and there is no obvious explanation for them or any one person as the direct culprit to blame. No one to point a finger at like Martha and Mary did.

If the pit you are in is a direct result from someone else's actions, then you need to find a way to forgive. You need to free up your feelings that have been keeping you in bondage and break away from that slavery. Releasing that pain and bitterness is not saying the actions didn't directly affect you in a negative way nor were they acceptable. You are certainly not justifying them. You are just not giving them any more space in your life or your heart and you are no longer allowing them to rob you. You are not allowing their actions to have authority over your life anyone. They have taken enough from you in the past so there is no reason to allow them to continue to take from your present or the future.

Do what you need to do to get past it. Write a letter to them describing all the pain, suffering and hurt that they caused you. Mail it to them or even burn it, flush it down the toilet or garbage disposal or tear it into a million pieces. Whatever you need to do to set them free from holding your life and heart captive any longer and finally breaking that chain of bondage that has held you hostage for so long, then do it. Take your heart and your future back!

If you are the direct cause of your addiction or your pit, then you need to seek help and you need to learn to forgive yourself. I highly suggest a pastor or a Christian counselor that can guide you in the right direction using the principles from the word of God. I am not against medical professionals, but many do not know how to help you with the spiritual aspect that is an integral part of healing and learning to live in the wholeness of Jesus.

Learning to forgive yourself is hard to do. I still live with feelings of guilt for what I put my husband and kids through. I hate the fact that I missed out on so much and the amount of emotional and financial struggle that I put on them. I did come to the realization that kids are resilient and that my spouse loves me as the Bible teaches us, so my degree of guilt is based on what I choose to do with it. It can hold me back and allow Satan to use it on me or I can choose to move on.

So, learn to forgive yourself. Not forgiving yourself is like trying to be a martyr for your actions and not allowing yourself to move forward. It is still living in the past. Pray, ask God to forgive you and leave it at the feet of Jesus. Not forgiving yourself is like telling Jesus that what he did on the cross was not enough and that you must bear the burden too. You have to pay your penance by wearing this cloak of shame around because you believe that it somehow makes you feel sorrier for your actions. No, it just reminds you and everyone else of what has happened. Learn to move on.

When God looks at you, he sees his child, created and formed by him. You see brokenness with cracks and splinters but the potter looks at the clay waiting to mold and shape into something beautiful and smooth all the rough parts out to be instrumental for him. He sees a warrior and a conqueror waiting to realize their potential as they look in the mirror. You see unforgivable and he sees his blood washed white as snow. You see no hope and death of life and lack of joy and he has resurrected to conquer all of that! So, who are you going to believe?

Life isn't fair but God is. He heals the brokenhearted. We have all turned away, fallen or been hurt at some point in our lives. But while we were down, away from God, pursuing other means of coping, happiness or just existing, God loved us. He continues to pursue us and he continues to give you life because he has a purpose for you.

That night when I was all alone and decided that I had nowhere else to go but to look inward deep inside myself, I knew. God just said, "come home." He didn't turn me away. He didn't go through the list of chances that He gave me to straighten up. He didn't refuse me. He picked me up off that floor and gave me love, purpose, and hope. I felt like I had to make the choice to choose Him because I had nothing else or any guarantees of what the outcome was going to be. That night in all actuality He had already chosen me. I just needed to realize it.

But back to the story with Lazarus. It didn't end with Mary and Martha crying to Jesus about being late. In John 11:39, "...Take ye away the stone..." Jesus moved that one thing that was keeping Lazarus from coming out of that grave. The stone! Jesus will remove whatever stone, boulder, rock, or mountain that you have in your life. You must be willing. Lazarus was dead and made alive behind that stone, but in order to actually life a life, the stone had to be moved. You must realize you can be made alive again, but you must be willing to allow God to move your stone. Your heart of stone.

That thing in your life that stands between you and him that keeps you from truly living. "And when thus he had spoken, he cried with a loud voice, Lazarus, come forth. And he that was dead came forth, bound hand and foot with graveclothes: and his face was bound about with a napkin. Jesus saith unto them, Loose him, and let him go." (John 11:43-44). See once you allow Jesus to move that stone you will never be the same. He's telling you to come forth and live just like he did Lazarus, but will you?

He loves you so much that he will not force himself on you but will do as John 6:37 says, "...and him that cometh to me, I will no wise cast thee out." He won't say no to your humble heart. I knew that night, in the psychiatric ward, that there were a lot of things not stable and secure in my life, but I knew all I had was Jesus. Many times, it is only in that rock-bottom pit when there is nowhere to look but up that many find help and healing. Some, however, try to dig their own way out. And just when they think progress is being made, the walls can cave in.

So maybe your story is nothing like mine but maybe you are shackled and a slave to yourself, your job, your emotions or even expectations that others place on you. I come to tell you that Christ is the giver of life and paid the price so that you may be free. He bore all of our sins, weaknesses, and bondage at Calvary. He came to break those chains and allow you to live free in Him. In order to live free, you must first admit there is a problem and that you are in fact shackled. It might not be as drastic as mine was or last for 13 years, but it is your story and that is personal and binding. It might be your secret sin that you keep tucked away to yourself that you can't seem to break the cycle or get passed it. Whatever it is, it is constantly keeping you bound and weighing on you.

Don't lose hope. Hope is not pretending like you don't have trouble. It is not keeping your head in the clouds. It is the hope and belief that the troubles will not last forever. That you can overcome the difficulties and the hurts will be healed. That you will be led out of the darkness. It is the still small voice of the Holy Spirit that is rooting for you and saying, "Keep on" and "Don't give up!" Don't listen to Satan telling you lies that are contrary.

"...but also, if ye shall say unto this mountain, Be thou removed, and be thou cast into the sea; it shall be done." (Matthew 21:21) That is powerful. That is making the choice to keep putting one foot in front of the other and believing in the power and love of God. It is knowing that climbing mountains will build strength to endure the top and appreciate the view. Then you can proclaim, "**I have fought a good fight, I have finished my course, I have kept the faith.**" (2 Timothy 4:7)

You can know that one day your crown will far outweigh any cross that you have had to bear in this life. Choose not to just hope in being a conqueror but choose to place your hope in the ultimate conqueror of death, hell, and the grave, and that is Jesus. Know that your hope completely outweighs any hardship that you may face. "If in this life only we have hope in Christ, we are of all men most miserable." (1 Corinthians 15:19) In those dark times in life when you feel defeated and spiraling down just look up and remember that God can be trusted.

That he has promised, "...I will never leave thee, nor forsake thee." (Hebrews 13:5)

The way that we handle our sufferings has the potential to silence Satan. It is like that bully at school. If they know that they are getting to us, they have control and the upper hand, and they will just keep attacking. They will chip little by little at us until we are defenseless, but the minute that we stand up to them and decide to stop taking the abuse and stand firm on our own two feet, they are blindsided and quickly back away. Stop letting Satan bully you. You are much stronger than you think because "Greater is he that in you than he that is in the world." (1 John 4:4). God's love and favor far outweigh your struggles, your emotions, and your battles. Claim this and believe it. "By this I know that thou favourest me, because mine enemy doth not triumph over me." (Psalm 41:11)

Have determination. It gives you the resolve to keep going despite any accusations or roadblocks that Satan might throw your way. Galatians 6:9 tells us, "And let us not be weary in well doing: for in due season we shall reap, if we faint not." The only chain breaker that there is is Jesus! Don't give up trying just GET UP from those chains and take yourself to the feet of the cross. That is the only place that you will find true peaceful lasting freedom.

Taking off that masquerade and being my true self was so scary and freeing at the same time. I had to choose to do it, and I didn't do it alone- God was my "...my deliverer, My God, my strength, in whom I will trust.." (Psalms 18:2) Fear can keep us from moving forward, but it can also keep us paralyzed in the position right where we are. Many live in fear that their dreams will never come true, relationships will never get mended, addictions will never be conquered or that living for God requires too much sacrifice and clean up. We resign ourselves to the fact that this is just how we will always be and the card that we have been dealt in this life.

But, isn't the risk worth the reward? Isn't fighting for yourself and those you love worth mustering up an ounce of courage and faith. Matthew 17:20 tells us that, "...If ye have faith as a grain of mustard seed, ye shall say unto this mountain, Remove hence to yonder place; and it shall remove; and nothing shall be impossible unto you." So get a tiny seed of faith, which is minuscule, and believe that there is more to life than what you are living and just try.

We all have "worst days" that have been etched in our minds, memory, and maybe even scarred our hearts. We may think things just can't ever get any better, but I am telling you that they can. Look at fear in a new way as this acronym "FACING EVERYTHING AND RISING." You have survived 100% of your worst days so far! You will survive this too. So, let's start telling those negative emotions, strongholds, memories, addictions, feelings, and fears that keep us weak - "But God!"

So maybe you have tried before-try again. It doesn't matter how many times you try don't give up. Elite athletes, famous composers, and even actors don't give up after their first failure. Abraham Lincoln was defeated in several different elections before succeeding. Thomas Edison was dubbed by one of his teachers as "too stupid to learn anything." Henry Ford went broke five times before he ever succeeded. Michael Jordan was cut from his high school team. Walt Disney was fired for having a lack of imagination. And the list goes on and on of people in life that have been coined as successful yet failed many times before getting it right. But how?

They didn't take no for an answer. The end result was bigger than the present failure. They pressed on. They persevered despite the setbacks. They claimed the victory of the war and looked beyond the present defeat of the battle. They aren't superhuman like we tend to think, putting them up on a pedestal. Many of them had humble beginnings and they knew the definition of work but also knew the definition of defeat. They didn't let the latter win. They didn't take no for an answer or an option.

We give ourselves to many options. We are often full of excuses and many times we have an essay in our mind prepared for the whys or why nots. Sometimes they are legitimate reasons on why something didn't work or couldn't. They look good on paper, but God doesn't deal with the easy. He specializes in doing things in a big way and to the fullest. He wants to do that in your life.

That little three letter word "but" is often a parent's most hated word because when we tell our kids to do something, they often times will fire back with "but why." Anyone that has been a parent to a young child that asks a million questions in a minute knows that "because I said so" is not sufficient for most of them. That 3-letter conjunction is used after a statement is proclaimed and leads into a statement that is contrary to the first.

As I was learning to live a new life without medications to cope or to take the edge off, I had to fill my mind and my heart with new things, factual things, concrete truth. Scripture is where I turned to. That verse that my sister put on the nightstand during my initial days of detox became my life verse, Psalm 73:26. As I would feel negative thoughts come into my mind or Satan would try to plant seeds of doubt, anxiousness or worry, I would just repeat and proclaim over and over, "My flesh and my heart may fail, BUT GOD is the strength of my heart and my portion forever." I knew that no matter what went wrong, what fell apart or how I may falter or fail if I would allow God to take over, He would be my strength and concrete foundation.

This little phrase "but God" is used over forty times in scripture. Maybe you allow yourself to have excuses or the way of hope is not obvious to you. No matter where you turn the journey is futile. The world says no- but God says yes. You may say can't- but God says can. Others may say, and you have convinced yourself, that you never will be able to and God says you will. The world and Satan may say stop and just give up, but God says go and keep trying! You decide who you are going to listen to and believe.

Life throws so many things at us and most of them are unplanned and unexpected. I could plan for all the terrible things that go wrong in our lives then I would never learn to depend on God. I would be depending on my own strength and then glorify myself for making it through. So, when your flesh fails, and you are weary from the day, or health issues attack and you feel like you can't carry on then claim, "But God." When your fleshly desires are bombarding you to give in to temptation or you have no energy or fight left then stop and claim the victory "But GOD is my strength." When your heart fails from brokenness or loneliness or gets hurt, stepped on or taken for granted or even if you lose your hope or faith recall the promise "But GOD is my strength and my portion forever."

By medical standards, I should not be alive right now typing these words or should have given in when I went cold turkey off my medicine because it was just too hard, but I tell all of them- but God. I should have never left the psychiatric ward in less than twenty-four hours after voluntarily signing a commit order. But I say-but God. I should still be suffering from debilitating anxiety and depression, yet I claim- but God. 1 Corinthians 2:9 tells us "But as it is written, Eye hath not seen, nor ear heard, neither have entered into the heart of man, the things which God hath prepared for them that love him."

Believing in the God of the universe and creator of all things is a much wiser decision no matter how hard the process may seem, how high the mountain may feel or how lonely the valley may be. Satan thought he had won when Jesus died on the Cross but that small three letter conjunction is our hope because the story didn't end in the tomb. "But God" raised Jesus up from the dead. *That* is our victory and *that* is our hope. So that word should not be used as an excuse in our lives, instead, it should be our victory cry and our faith that our strongholds will no longer hold strong in our lives.

I had to start believing in my present and my future and stop letting Satan throw up my past to keep me from moving forward. When I really began, not only reading the scripture but believing the scriptures, my heart began to change, and my attitude and actions followed. I really understood for once that I was not alone. It does not mean that I, nor you, will never struggle again because Satan is still trying to sift us like wheat, but we have an advocate and we can tell Satan" But God."

Tell your doubts, worries, and fears and you might even have to tell your haters, "but God." We all know that people get jealous when you decide to branch out, prosper or gain momentum. Some may even try to sabotage your progress or your victory because it may remind them of their defeats. Misery loves company. Be aware that Satan will use anything and anyone to win. If he can keep you down, then he has won. I wish we would just get holy anger on what he does and tries to do in our lives. We need to put on our armor and battle *with* our Heavenly Father knowing that Satan is coming and be adamant that we will not let him win. You tell him ok, I got you and I know what you are up to, "but God" has me.

I was concerned before I ever began to write, what others would think about all the secrets that I was bringing into the light. I am not advocating that you go and air all your dirty laundry, and especially not on social media, but with much time in prayer and conversations with my family, I felt that keeping my story silent was keeping a burden buried and a victory restrained. I realized Satan liked the fact that I was still hiding behind the masquerade of lies, deception and most of all shame. It may have not been in the same aspect as medication and depression any longer, but it was still hiding. It was keeping my story silent. It was choosing to keep my testimony and the redeeming grace and forgiveness of Jesus hid. It was choosing to still live in defeat rather than claiming the complete victory.

When I came to grips with this fear and I said "But God" is when the words began to flow, and the story could be told. I no longer hide behind my masquerade and I choose to tell all the lies that Satan throws at me -But God.

# The Mask Isn't Worth It

When a person goes to a masquerade ball, they pick out their outfit with careful consideration, but most of the emphasis and focus is placed on the mask. It's what everyone sees first and notices, the differences that are unique to each person and personality. Some are just black and white, some are flashy with sequins and feathers, and others are a combination of both. Battling a mental issue is not a choice that anyone in their right mind would pick but the degree in which one suffers is very different and unique to each person, just like the masks. Some battle only during certain seasons with depression while others have debilitating anxiety that hinders their everyday livelihood.

Just as unique as the mask can be, so are the triggers, symptoms, and degrees in which one may suffer. I do not make light or dismiss the fact that mental health issues are real and very hard battles to deal with. I do not negate the validity of mental health issues and the suffering that so many go through as I did. I do not believe that you can just pray every mental health issue away, but I do personally believe in putting in the work to better the situation and the outcome.

I believe that we have three parts, the physical, emotional, and spiritual. All three must be dealt with. They are interwoven together. The physical part can be checked by a healthcare professional checking levels of hormones, vitamins and actual scientific medical issues that can be proven with blood tests. Proper sleep, nutrition, and exercise can and will directly affect everyone and not always in the short term seeing instant effects whether positive or negative but maybe in the long term. The emotional side of who we are may need to be evaluated whether dealing with anxiety or panic. When either or both set in, stop and analyze if you are listening to the truth or focusing on all the uncontrollable matters that may never come to pass. Seeking counseling from a trained professional can help guide you, in ways that can be effective, to stabilize your emotions. It's learning to self-talk and recite positive affirmations of truth about who you are, not who you are not, or what you have done. The spiritual part of who we are requires checkups too. Maintaining proper habits of prayer and bible study and believing that God wants to renew our minds. Not just reading our Bible and agreeing with all the good promises but actually believing them and living them out.

Anything out of balance is not working properly. I don't want to step on a scale that has chipped and faulty weights. Who does? If the weights are too heavy, then it gives a false reading saying that I weigh more than I do. That will really cause some depression; however, if the weights are too light, I get all excited giving me false happiness and joy. Everything must be in check and register properly to give a true and accurate reading.

We are the same way. All three components of who we are must be in balance. If just one is slightly off, then it throws all three out of harmony. That's just how easy it is for depression and anxiety to take over your life. Instead of you living and dictating to them when they rear their ugly heads, they then begin to consume and dictate to you. We have to get back into balanced living. Physical, emotional and spiritual were created to work together not to fight against each other.

So no, I do not believe, that you can just pray everything away all the time because if that were true, then my battles would not have taken thirteen years to go away. I had to learn how to live with balance and understanding and realize when things are off balance to stop and evaluate before I react. You can't just treat symptoms, you must get down to the cause and the root issue. Are your sleep patterns off? Have you been sick? Has your schedule been too busy? Are you reading your Bible? Are you putting garbage in your mind because that will allow garbage to come out?

Taking medicine to help you is not what I am against. I am against taking medicine and not working on the other aspects to help along with the medicine. I am against using it as a magic pill to fix things and not putting our own work to check our habits. Treating only one aspect of who we are is like sitting in a car expecting it to go on its own. You have to have the keys or the key fob and there must be gas in the car. If just one of the aspects, whether it be you, the key or the gas are not present then that car is not going to go. They all three must exist for it run and drive as intended. So, if you are just taking medicine, and doing nothing else to help your mental health strategy then you are not running as intended. You are your best advocate and the good news is that God wants to be right alongside you to make you whole.

So maybe you aren't the one directly suffering from mental health battles or addictions, but someone close to you is. Love them. Pray for them. It can be hard to know what the right thing to do in helping someone. Listen to them. It's not always the words that they say but the actions behind the words that are sometimes not spoken. Just being there without judgment. You don't always have to fix things or have the perfect advice. Just being there for them speaks volumes. Encouraging them to talk and to not hide behind the mask, hurt or pain is so very helpful. Let them know that whatever they say will not be received with judgment but with love and true concern.

Addictions, depression, and anxiety can make you feel alone even in a crowd. Being present, sending messages and just friendly interaction can cause them to feel normal and not isolated. Isolation and feelings that no one understands what you are going through is very common and sometimes no matter what words you say nothing will change that, but your presence can be a motivating factor into alternative thinking. Finally, don't dismiss their feelings. No matter what you say, even if it's grounded in truth, it must be filtered before you say it to them. Telling them things like "cheer up" or "just pray" will not automatically win you on their side to open up and jump at the chance to get better. It might just backfire on you and cause more division. Not every foundational doctrine and scripture needs to be recited to them. Learn to talk WITH them and NOT at them.

Wearing a masquerade allows one to hide not only from themselves, but they believe they are hiding from others. I did. I never realized how many people actually noticed how much I had become like a zombie because of the heavy medication. I never comprehended or recalled having conversations where my speech was slurred or my eyes were glassy, but they were. I didn't see that when I looked at myself because the mask was on, but others did. So, if you are suffering, don't be fooled into thinking that others don't know, they do. If you are hiding, don't be fooled into thinking that others don't care, because they do. Learn to take the mask off so you can put in the work to heal completely balancing out all three areas of your life, the physical, emotional and the spiritual. If you have someone in your life that battles, be the soft place they can land if they fall and allow them to show you the raw, un-doctored and messy person behind the mask without judgment and nothing but love.

The mask isn't worth wearing because it hinders your healing and that will only come with honesty!

# The Music Plays On

I remember learning how to drive. My dad wanted us to learn how to drive a standard. He felt that you needed to know just in case of an emergency and that was the only car left in the driveway. He didn't want someone dying on me because I couldn't drive the car. We left our neighborhood and went on some old country roads so he could teach me how to drive the standard. He got out and patiently described to me how to slowly release off the clutch and simultaneously start pushing on the gas. I was pretty coordinated as a dancer for many years so my right and left feet could do different things at different times. I learned like a pro. I had it all down pat.

It came time for me to get my license and my first vehicle, of course, it was a standard. It was an old blue Chevette with rust building up on the hood already, so you know it wasn't anything fancy, but it was mine. I was so excited that I called all my friends on our house phone to see if I could pick them up for school the next morning. I was carpooling with my friends and I wanted to be the driver. I was eagerly wanting to cruise around with all my friends in my own car.

It was the very first day that I was given permission to drive my car to school. That morning I had arranged to pick up a few of my very best friends. One specific girlfriend lived in a small neighborhood on the way to school and I headed to her house after picking up one other. There were now three of us in my rusty blue standard Chevette headed to school. I didn't consider the morning traffic, nor did I think things through when I decided which street to take out of her neighborhood and onto the main road.

It was a street with a major incline or hill to get out of the neighborhood and back onto the main street. There were cars everywhere. I just took a deep breath in and slowly tried releasing and gassing as my dad had taught me to do but the car died. It died again and again. At this point, I am getting embarrassed and was beginning to panic a little. The line of cars behind me was piling up. I didn't know what else to do as my friends were not understanding my dilemma and just saying over and over to just go. I couldn't just let my car roll down the hill and then gas it like I wanted to because of the cars that were lined up behind me.

So, I let the car die one final time, I put my foot on the brake and rolled down my window. I stuck my arm out the window and waved everyone around me. I just pretended like I was having mechanical issues. I couldn't look up and I didn't look around as one by one the cars began pulling around me. I kept looking in the rear-view mirror counting the cars that were left to pass me. It was now all clear. I waited just a moment, took a deep breathe again and it was still clear. I turned the key in the ignition. I revved the engine, let the old blue Chevette slightly roll down the hill and I gassed it. I prayed no cars were coming on the main road as I flew out into it, gliding on two wheels. We made it safely. We were all laughing at this point. I just turned up the radio ignoring all the things that had just occurred.

I am not so sure that I could punch it up a hill with a standard anymore, but the concept of driving is something we do each day without even thinking about it. It has become second nature and the rules, regulations, and processes that it requires from the time that you get in your car, put on your seatbelt, and turn on the ignition to get you to your destination have become second nature. I no longer have to think through each step methodically as my daddy introduced driving to me on that old country road.

Living with a masquerade and insecurities can very much be the same way. We don't even think about what truth is anymore. Living a defeated life has become our habit and our second nature. When we wake up in the morning, it is there. When we lay our head down at night, it is still there. We can hear truth and even Biblical truth and we can agree with that truth wholeheartedly but believing in the truth and applying it are polar opposites. I could hear it, and, on some occasions, I even taught it to others, but allowing it to saturate my heart and mind and change my thinking was incomprehensible. We must stop just rolling down the hill and punch the gas into truth and reality.

We must silence the lies and stop returning to them as second nature or our go to's. We must swim up the stream in our hearts fighting against the flow that we have gotten comfortable in. We must fight the urges to revert to the familiar thoughts, habits, and ways that we have always done. We must stop letting others just go by us while we sit idly by waiting for the all clear because it's a risk and may never come.

"And be not conformed to this world: but be ye transformed by the renewing of your mind, that ye may prove what is that good, and acceptable, and perfect, will of God." (Romans 12:2) Transformed means to change composition- the makeup. What are you filling your mind with? What are the thoughts, ideas, and beliefs foundationally grounded on? Are they factual and by whose standards? Renewing is a process, making extensive changes or rebuilding. What has formed your thoughts about yourself, your situation or generated the habit of you wearing the masquerade?

This is the journal entry that I want to share from February 12, 2002, showing my mindset.

> *Why do I suffer in silence? Why do I allow the simple things of today to overwhelm me? I try to be superwoman and carry all the burdens on myself. I allow something so small to trigger me and I blow up. I don't allow God to use me and calm me. I allow Satan to use my weakness and to overcome me. If I would just settle down and reach for the Lord, it would make everything better. I need to rest in Him. I could relax in His peace and delight in His joy. I would be a much calmer person. I would enjoy life through Jesus more not despite Him. He lives in me and I need to live it.*

"...to him that knoweth to do good, and doeth it not, to him it is sin." (James 4:17) Stop driving your thoughts into the conformity of the world. Stop believing the lies, stop going back to what you have always done that is natural and learn how to renew your mind. Punch the gas and realize that you need to transform your heart, mind, attitude, and thinking. That takes effort and work but staying the way things are or have always been should not be an option in your life.

Renewing is a transitive verb. That means it has two characteristics. It is first an action verb expressing a doable act and second, it must have a direct object, something or someone who receives the action of the verb. With this concept, it is a process of restoring and refreshing your thoughts about yourself and how you project that towards your relationship with God. This requires work and action on your part. If you want to just keep rolling down the hill of life, and never get on the main road to your desired destination, then just keep doing it the way that you are and watch others continue to pass you by. However, if you really want to start laughing, turn up the volume and enjoy the ride and roll down that hill for the last time, just punch the gas propelling yourself forward and become who God intended you to be. He will navigate you towards his destination for your life, but you must be willing to be transformed by him.

Sometimes we can punch the gas on our own but sometimes it requires someone else to come along and give us a nudge in the right direction because the fog has rolled in and we really can't see where we are headed. I required that nudge from my family and more specifically my husband. The intervention that my family had for me was a small step for me. It, at least, took off the emergency brake, but then my husband's ultimatum was the real nudge. It was a jolt into reality onto the main road. I no longer hold any bitterness, resentment or hurt from his decision. He did the only thing he knew to do to propel me into reality and to clear the fog. Today I am thankful for it because it saved my life.

The other issue that I had to face to accelerate my healing forward was to finally put my grief behind me. I will forever be sad and miss my mom. She was one of a kind, a matchless Nana, and truly the purest example of a Proverbs 31 woman that will ever be, but I had anger hidden deep inside. I was angry that she did not take care of herself as I felt she could, that she left this Earth way to early and that my oldest has limited memories of her and my youngest has none. I harbored those feelings for many years and one day I just wrote her a letter and told her how I felt. I told her I missed her, that I still needed her, but most of all I wished she could see me now. That she could see that I made it. That day in the hospital I told her I would be okay just to soothe her mind never really believing it myself but here I am today living it out. I am more okay and at peace then I could ever have imagined. I wish I could share it with her but the peace that I have is that one day we will worship God and praise Him together. He is the one who loved me and showed me the grace to keep my promise I made to her that last day that I spoke to her. That promise was not broken.

Stop believing the lies and stop living in silence. Stop holding on to those things that you are afraid of, hurt from, or embarrassed about. They become a weight and we begin to worship those with the consumption of our time, neglecting our Savior. They have consumed all our time, attention and allegiance for far too long.

"How are you doing?" is the usual verbiage used in greeting someone. "Great or Fine" is our customary response. Knowing good and well those words sting coming out of our lips. I learned to say, "do you want me to tell you the truth or lie to you." I knew, even struggling all those years, that no one wanted to be bored with my sappy and grueling details of how bad my day was going. I just stood there smiling and appearing to have it all together while on the inside my heart was spinning like a tornado and tearing into pieces wanting to scream, "Help!"

Many people suffer from either mental or physical ailments and a lot of times those two come hand in hand and no one ever knows anything about it. They suffer in silence due to the embarrassment and stigma that their situation, diagnosis, addiction, or disease brings. They suppress feelings all the while appearing to have everything under control as if everything is fine knowing good and well that it's not. They don't share struggles, worries, burdens or any emotions because they feel that it would consume all conversations forward. They certainly don't want to be defined or labeled any more than they already have been by the diagnosis, others or even themselves. All they really want is to be SEEN and to be HEARD.

This has been my story, my journey, and my victory. Too many people suffer in silence, especially in a church setting because of the stigma that is placed on mental illness and addictions. It is both unfair and unnecessary.

Yet, why is there an embarrassment? Adam and Eve were looking for more. They justified their actions and placed the blame on the serpent taking no responsibility for their own actions. Matthew 22:37 commands us, "Thou shalt love the Lord thy God with all thy heart, and with all thy soul, and with all thy mind." That is a personal responsibility. It is your job to keep your own heart guarded and in a right relationship with God. Shalt is a present tense verb and that means now and with action. You can't keep blaming your past and living there and expecting any different outcome in the present or for the future. Albert Einstein stated that "Insanity is doing the same thing over and over and expecting a different result." So, in order to love God with all your heart, soul and mind it takes action. Action on your part, with a purpose in mind, to walk one step closer every day to becoming who God created you to be, with vigilant prayer, and Bible study and that will allow you to take steps away from the lies that Satan is bombarding your mind with about who you are. You need to take steps away from the negativity and destructive behaviors in your life. Find a new normal with God.

The next verses are so very personal to me. In verse 39 it states, "And the second is like unto it, Thou shalt love thy neighbor as thyself." Just one time I wish someone would have asked me how I was doing, and I had the assurance that it was okay to spill my heart without any judgment or embarrassment. We all want to be accepted and loved without having to strategically clean ourselves up or appear to have it all together all the time. None of us want to be judged, ridiculed or have expectations placed on us that are not sensible. So, if we don't want that done to us then why do we do it others?

Churches should be a safe place for sinners, a hospital of healing, a support system for the weak and a soft place to land for the weary and worn yet many feel that they can't even walk thru the doors without going thru a "judgment protector" waiting for them at the door. It would be like a metal detector that would beep as they cross the threshold of the entrance of the church sounding the alarm that something is wrong with this person. They feel as if it will just sound an alarm spilling every crack in their character or every sin that they have submitted to. Why is it when we ask for prayer requests that we can't ask for the true burdens on our hearts that are truly weighing us down outside the walls of the sanctuary? May we learn to see people and not just bodies. May we see eyes and not just pupils. That there are feelings and hearts behind that flesh and dreams and visions and fears behind those blue, green, brown or hazel circles that are crying out in need for someone to notice them. Someone to care.

Social media has all our bests on display as a highlight reel. We don't post about the tireless nights up with sick kids or the bills coming in the mail. We post the picture-perfect world where everything is good and right. Yet, we all struggle. Some do more than others and on any given day, it could be us if we aren't already. I often tell my boys when people are downright rude or ugly to think about what they may be going thru behind closed doors at home. Not even always at home but in someone's heart or head, the warfare that they may be facing. That we all face.

Don't judge someone if they post their really bad day on social media and surely don't judge someone asking for help, prayer or the fact that they may look like they slept in their clothes and haven't bathed in days because that just may be the reality for them. You, my friend, are not called to unjustly judge, fix or analyze. You are called to love. So, love those who need to be loved and hug those who just need to be hugged. But the biggest and most heartwarming thing that you can do is pray with them and ask them what you can specifically pray for.

I am not saying that any of this would have made a complete difference or stopped my 13 years of struggles but if we could be more aware of ourselves and others and truly love as Jesus did without judgment, hesitation and with open arms, then it might just be what someone else needs to realize who they are in Christ and how healing can begin and hope to carry on.

My prayer through all these writings is that if anyone reading this is hiding behind their struggles that they may come to realize that you CAN'T GIVE YOURSELF OPTIONS. The only option you have is Jesus and for those of us who call ourselves Christians and want to be like Christ remember. DON'T GIVE YOURSELF OPTIONS to judge others but to JUST LOVE!

My struggle has and will always be the fact that I am a people pleaser and living as if love is performance driven. Struggles are real, doubts are weighing, and fears are debilitating. You may not struggle with the same thing. You may have health issues, relationship stresses, financial difficulties or internal turmoil. You may not have any of them at the present moment but get ready you will face one of them in the future, maybe each of them, and it might be all of them at once.

You may show the strength of a lion or cower down as defenseless as a sheep but either way, the struggle is there. No one is immune. It does not show prejudice or favorites and we are warned in scripture. (John 16:33) "These things I have spoken unto you, that in me ye might have peace. In the world ye shall have tribulation: but be of good cheer; I have overcome the world." So, decide now in your heart that you will not let it defeat you. You will be the lion with the courage from Christ, but on the flip side, you will be the lamb with a gentle, humble, teachable spirit from our Savior as well.

So, what are you going to settle? Settle in the fact that this is the way life is always going to be. Hidden behind your hurts, fears, bitterness, and pain, or to break free from the labels. If I would have settled for the medical norm then I would still be highly medicated, in and out of treatment centers, suicidal and still hiding in silence. The masquerade would still be in place and who I was would be still be dictated to me by the world's standards. I want to settle in truth and know that being silent about struggles no matter how big or little only suppresses true feelings. Suppressed feelings turn into denial and denial turns into never admitting or accepting that there is an issue. So, help is not received for healing. If Jesus is not Lord over everything including the hidden secrets, the layers upon layers of hidden things behind your masquerade, then he might be your Savior, but you are not letting him be Lord over all.

So, I am choosing to settle in facts and get comfortable living and believing "but God." That my flesh and my heart may fail. I might be depressed or be filled with anxiety at some other time in my life, but I can say he is the strength of my portion forever. This is an excerpt all the way back from 2002 in one of my journals and it is as if I had written these words today giving hope to myself.

> *The hardest thing is putting the past behind. I hold it as a measuring stick for the future. I compare it to the present*

> *and doubt my success. I will give up on the future because of the past. I know that the past is gone. I need to leave it gone. I can succeed. I can accomplish my goals and achieve them taking one step at a time. One day at a time. I will make mistakes, but they don't have to be so detrimental to my life. I need to pick up and keep going. God holds the day in his hand. He gives me the self-discipline and endurance to go on. His supply never runs out-so mine shouldn't either.*

The mask is off, the silence is broken, and my ball continues to go on, but I hear a much different tune now in my life. It is a beautiful love song from my Savior saying that He will never leave me nor forsake me. That I am fearfully and wonderfully made and that I can be strong and have good courage because I will face trouble in the future, but I don't have to fear evil because he will personally comfort me. He has overcome the world and when those trials, doubts, fears and negative feelings start stirring that I can tell them all "but God."

So, as I wash my face day and night and allow the warm water to cover my skin, some days the residue of the old masquerade tries to creep up. Looking in the mirror, Satan tries to tell me to hide, to put on that masquerade and to just close my mouth in shame. I rub and rub with cleanser the truth of God's word-washing away all the hurt, the pain, and the lies that Satan projects onto me, and I stand there refreshed reminded that God loves me just as I am.

I know that life is hard, but God is good. No matter what you or I are going through mere words won't make the journey any easier and they won't make things go away but the touch from above can and will. God gives us a new day every single morning with the sun rising. A new day to choose who we will be, how we will act and react. A day to choose to no longer wear a masquerade. Instead, a name tag or a billboard in lights that say forgiven and redeemed. I don't wear a masquerade any longer and I now pray as I have been transparent, raw, unfiltered and myself with all the good, bad, and gory details that the person I want people to see and remember is that this is me. My prayer is that one might not see any of the good that I have done but that they can say, "...I have seen thy face, as though I had seen the face of God, and thou wast pleased with me." (Genesis 33:10)

Printed in the USA
CPSIA information can be obtained
at www.ICGtesting.com
LVHW030743010823
753891LV00032B/118